Brazil–China Relations in the 21st Century

Maurício Santoro

Brazil–China Relations in the 21st Century

The Making of a Strategic Partnership

Maurício Santoro
Department of International Relations
State University of Rio de Janeiro
Rio de Janeiro, Brazil

ISBN 978-981-19-0355-7   ISBN 978-981-19-0353-3   (eBook)
https://doi.org/10.1007/978-981-19-0353-3

This Palgrave Macmillan imprint is published by the registered company Springer Nature
Singapore Pte Ltd.
The registered company address is: 152 Beach Road, #21-01/04 Gateway East, Singapore
189721, Singapore

To my nieces and nephew, Alice de Souza Santoro, Camille Facina de Oliveira Santoro and Pedro de Souza e Silva. May your journey through this century may be full of wonder and adventure.

ACKNOWLEDGMENTS

This book is an unexpected result of the pandemic, a fruit of turbulent times. But it is also the product of a network of support and solidarity. Jacob Dyer invited me to write it after he read an interview that Emma Graham-Harrison and Tom Phillips did with me about Brazil-China relations, on the British newspaper *The Guardian*. Thank you for believing in the potential of the idea, Jacob, and for the support of the Palgrave MacMillan team during the process.

I interviewed several people for this book—businessmen, diplomats, journalists, military officers, scientists and scholars. They shared with me their time, passions and interests about China. I thank Ana Cândida Perez, Celso Amorim, Charles Tang, Gilberto Câmara, Jaime Spitcovsky, Luiz Augusto Castro Neves, Margaret Myers, Milena de Moura, Natalie Unterstell, Paulo Menechelli, Paulo Roberto da Silva Gomes Filho, Qiao Jinzghen, Tatiana Prazeres and Welber Barral for their kindness and support. The quotes I use in this work are but a sample of their deep knowledge on China.

Over the years, I engaged in many dialogues with colleagues from Brazil, China, the United States and other countries. Many of them were important to this book due to their analysis, observations and suggestions. I am especially grateful to Adriana Abdenur and Maiara Folly (Plataforma CIPÓ), André Bueno and Elisa Corrêa (State University of Rio de Janeiro), Carol Wise (University of Southern California),

Elizabeth Knup (Ford Foundation), Evan Feigenbaum (Carnegie Endowment for International Peace), Jonathan Watts (*The Guardian*), Julia Leite and Cinthia Hoskinson (Centro Brasileiro de Relações Internacionais), Juliana Barbassa (New York Times) and Luiza Duarte (American University/Woodrow Wilson Center for International Scholars) for their contributions.

The staff at Observa China and Plataforma Shumian—especially the Chinese book club—have been great partners in the quest for developing a group of Brazilian scholars dedicated to understanding China and what its rise means to Brazil. I thank Igor Patrick, Julia Rosa, Lívia Machado Costa, Talita Fernandes and Thiago Bessimo for countless hours of good conversation and friendship.

Several journalists interviewed me about China during the writing of this book, giving me the opportunity to share these ideas with a large audience and test some of the concepts that I use in the text. My thanks to Andrew Rossetti (Bloomberg), Catherine Osborn (Foreign Policy), Carolina Morand, Marcelo Ninio and Roberto Maltchik (*O Globo*), Emma Graham-Harrison and Tom Phillips (*The Guardian*), Flávia Milhorance and Manuela Andreoni (Dialogo Chino), Guga Chacra and Marcelo Lins (GloboNews), Gustavo Ribeiro (Brazilian Report), João Paulo Charleaux (Nexo Jornal), João Pedro Malar (CNN Brazil), Petria Chaves (Rádio CBN), Sarah Maslin (*The Economist*), Thiago Amâncio (*Folha de São Paulo*), Zhao Yan and Chen Weihua (Xinhua) and Xiaomiao Shi (China Radio International).

My students at the State University of Rio de Janeiro have been incredibly enthusiastic and supportive of this project, especially the graduate school members who took my course on Brazil-China relations: Astrid Cazalbón, Beatriz Santos, Bruna Freixo, Igor Vilela, Matheus dos Santos, Nathan Morais and Octavio Oliveira. I incorporated many of their questions and ideas in the following chapters.

My colleages at the Mandarin course have been kind and curious concern my work, and I thank to my teachers, Liou Sheaujiuan and Wang Yili, for the community they have been built over the years.

Several friends read some of the chapters and helped me with suggestions and corrections. Fernando Paiva, Filipe Porto, Monique Sochaczweski Goldfeld and Pablo Ibanez were especially dedicated. Doctor Alfredo Pasin took good care of my health during the hard times of the pandemic and gave me fundamental support to carry this project.

Last but not least, my family was there for me. My father Ruy Ferreira Rocha, my mother Wanda Santoro Rocha, my brother Márcio Santoro Rocha and my sister-in-law Fernanda Souza Santoro heard several of the stories of this book and shared with me the joys and efforts of the work. My deep thank you to all of them.

INTRODUCTION

My father was born in a small town in the Amazon, Marabá. Recently, he told me: "When I was a child in 1940s, I never dreamed that one day I would have a son who studies Mandarin and researches China." And yet, my dad's hometown is receiving billions of dollars of Chinese investment in railways and steel plants, as a regional mining and transportation hub. It is a symbol of the journey of the Sino-Brazilian relations in the last decades. China is now key to Brazil's economic welfare, whether one lives in Brasília, Rio de Janeiro, São Paulo or Marabá.

This book is an analysis of the relationship between Brazil and China in the twenty-first century, a case study on how two of the biggest countries of the Global South are building what they called a "strategic partnership"—the term, invented by their diplomats in the 1990s, is in itself an attempt to frame a bilateral agenda that both nations perceived to be crucial for their long-term diplomatic perspectives although not in the traditional way of, let's say, a military alliance.

The Sino-Brazilian strategic partnership has been built around two main lines of actions: joint efforts to promote economic development and multilateral collaboration in search of a multipolar world. The dialogue between Beijing and Brasília began in 1974, when Brazil recognized the People's Republic of China (PRC), and it started to reach its full potential in the 2000s, during the global commodity boom, when trade grew and China became Brazil's biggest trade partner, buying its soybeans, iron ore and oil.

In the 2010s, Chinese firms became major investors in Brazil, especially in electrical energy and oil. They enjoyed an open and stable juridical framework, without the obstacles that they would meet in many countries of the Global North, and benefited from political goodwill from Brasília due to the strategic partnership.

These economic trends were part of a larger pattern concerning China and Latin America, but Brazil always was in a special position because of its size and its diplomatic importance to Beijing. Trade and investments regarding commodities are crucial to the bilateral relationship, but it also goes far beyond that, with a level of complexity unknown to other nations in the region in their dealing with the PRC. The Sino-Brazilian strategic partnership includes, for example, a joint program to build satellites, dialogues in multilateral groups such as BRICS, G20, BASIC and a rising agenda concerning the Amazon and climate change.

However, this strategic partnership is often a long and winding road. China's rise has been accompanied by a much more erratic development trajectory in Brazil, with several recessions and political crisis, episodes of hyperinflation and years of low economic growth. For many Brazilians, Chinese markets, capital and international cooperation are an opportunity to overcome these problems.

But for others, China is also part of the challenges that Brazil faces, especially regarding an industry without many capacities to compete abroad or even domestically against cheaper Chinese goods. An asymmetric pattern of trade seems to reinforce Brazilian dependency on the export of commodities.

There expectations, tensions and fears are exacerbated by the huge cultural distance that separates Brazil and China. As the author's father, many Brazilians are surprised, and sometimes afraid, about how Beijing's decisions impact in their daily lives. They also wonder on how the conflicts between China, United States and Europe will impact in Latin America, historically much closer to the West than to Asia.

The following pages tell the stories of many Brazilians and Chinese trying to learn how to work with each other. Sometimes they succeed, and sometimes they fail. They are artists, businesspeople, diplomats, journalists, military officers, politicians, scientists, scholars fascinated, worried, interested or repulsed by what they found in the country on the far side of their world. They negotiate trade deals, establish academic and scientific exchange programs, learn foreign languages, write dispatches and books, engage in complex diplomatic dialogues, buy goods or decide to invest.

With thousands of actions, they are building one of the most important bilateral relations between developing countries, with global impacts.

This book is divided into five chapters. The first one explains why the Brazilian military dictatorship, strongly anticommunist, decided to recognize the People's Republic of China when Mao Zedong was its president. The chapter tells the story of how this diplomatic relationship evolved from the 1970s to the 2000s, with the beginning of high-level visits, an ambitious scientific program to build satellites and the creation of the innovative concept of strategic partnership.

Chapters 2 and 3 deal with economic issues: trade and investments, respectively. In both chapters, there is an initial section with an overview of China's exchanges with Latin America, to highlight the similarities and differences with Brazil. Regarding trade, the text presents and analyzes the data for the bilateral relationship in the last 50 years, showing how a China hungry for food and raw materials stimulated a global commodity boom which transformed it in the Brazilian biggest economic partner. The text discusses how Brazil's agribusiness sector grew in response to China's demand. This is a case study on soybeans, the most important product in the bilateral economic exchange.

Concerning investments, Chapter 3 discusses what Chinese companies look for in Brazil, how they operate in the country and their main characteristics. The case study is on electrical energy, the sector that concentrates half of China's investments in Brazil. There is also a section on Brazilian investments in the Chinese market, questioning why they are small and the problems faced by Brazil's companies in their quest of internationalization in the Asian country.

Chapter 4 deals with China's role in the Amazon and how Beijing and Brasília are cooperating in a more assertive diplomacy to fight climate change. The text begins introducing the economic history of the Amazon, analyzing its several stages in the colonial times, in the military regime and in the recent democratic governments, explaining how the region became Brazil's biggest producer of meat and an important area for soybeans.

It then discusses the impacts of Chinese trade and investment in the Amazon, both in the positive and in the negative aspects. For example, there are bad consequences in terms of deforestation but also good measures in environmental responsibility, such as attempts to create systems of international certification to ensure that Chinese firms are not buying commodities that are products of illegal deforestation.

The last chapter of the book examines how the bilateral relationship with China became in recent years a subject of partisan polarization in Brazil, in face of the rise a nationalist right which seeks alignment with United States and see the Chinese Communist Party as an ideological threat and national security menace. The chapter discusses their criticism of China and how it became a source of tension for the diplomatic relations between both nations, especially during the coronavirus pandemic.

PRAISE FOR *BRAZIL–CHINA RELATIONS IN THE 21ST CENTURY*

"In the mid-seventies, Brazil's right-wing dictatorship, fresh from destroying a maoist insurgency, established diplomatic ties with Mao's China. By then, Chinese communists were interested in learning from Brazil's industrialization strategy without running into the same bottlenecks that locked Brazil in the "middle-income trap". Almost thirty years later, a China-fueled commodities boom helped Brazil's anti-poverty efforts achieve extraordinary results. Another fifteen years go by, and now Brazil is ruled by a far-right president who uses China-bashing to fire up its base. Throughout this whole story, Brazil is still in the middle-income trap, China is still ruled by the Communist Party, and both countries are interlocked in investment projects in the Amazon. Santoro's book provides extraordinary insight into how this story of globalization built from the south unfolded, and the problems that may emerge from it."

—Celso Rocha de Barros, *Political columnist at Folha de São Paulo*

"This is a reference book for those interested in the relationship between China and Brazil in the 21st century. Professor Santoro masterfully narrates such historical facts, pointing out political, diplomatic, cultural, and economic dimensions, contributing to a broader perception of this bilateral relationship. Summing up, this is an extremely relevant book, since China has for more than a decade been Brazil's main trade partner and, in the last one, Brazil's largest foreign investor."

—Dr. Thauan Santos, *Professor of Economics at the Brazilian Naval War College, Brazil*

"This important book is a real trail-opener in covering Sino-Brazilian modern relationship. With a fluent prose and several significant interviews, it allows the reader a full view of the subject, covering political, economic and social issues. Santoro's contribution is surely to influence present and future academic debates regarding how China and Brazil interact, as well as how this affects other interested countries."

—Professor Wellington Dantas de Amorim, *Brazilian Naval Academy, Brazil*

"Maurício Santoro is a keen observer of China. His book arrives at an opportune time. Even with the 2020 diplomatic disputes between a more ideological sphere of the current Brazilian government and the Chinese Minister of Foreign Affairs, the Asian giant continued to prosper in our territory. This presence is the result of a solid history of partnerships and large international projects, such as the BRICS. Santoro managed to shed some light on this narrative, ranging from the diplomatic foundations of this relationship until current times and its most complex challenges, such as the construction of an environmental agenda during the political turmoil in Brazil. This is a must-read for anyone interested in the growing Chinese role, not just in Brazil, but also in Latin America."

—Pablo Ibañez, *Professor of Geography and International Relations, Federal Rural University of Rio de Janeiro, Brazil*

"Professor Santoro has brought his uniquely incisive, conversational and approachable brand of academic research to this fascinating book. I have always been bowled over by his wide reading and seemingly infinite reserves of perspective on issues and ideas all and sundry. His empathetic genius is vindicated in this novel text on Brazil-China relations. I am very glad to see his excellent ideas collated and presented for the wider academic and public community. An unmissable text!"

—Devika Misra, *Professor of International Relations, O.P. Jindal Global University, India*

"Maurício Santoro's timely book captures the complexity of the evolving dynamic of the Brazil-China relations. He traces an insightful roadmap to understand the substance of this partnership in the last decades and points toward new potential trajectories to connect the two nations in a context of geopolitical power shifts."

—Luíza Duarte, *Global fellow at the Brazil Institute, Woodrow Wilson Center for International Scholars and at the American University in Washington, DC, USA*

"In times of an intensifying rivalry between the United States and China, middle powers like Brazil need guidance to navigate turbulent waters, especially after China overcame the United States as key trade partners of multiple nations. Using a fluid narrative and objective data, Santoro's book provides an insightful analysis of not only current China-Brazil relations but the making of a more multipolar order as well. The chapters on commodities trade, energy and infrastructure investments, and climate diplomacy are specially welcomed to both students and practitioners wishing to understand what is at stake in the making of this strategic - albeit sometimes difficult – partnership."

—Erica Resende, *Brazilian War College, Brazil*

"A vivid, insightful exploration of a relationship heavy with lessons about development and strategic goals in a multipolar world—from one of the scholars who knows the relationship best. Maurício Santoro guides readers through the actors, interests, debates, and tensions that make up Brazil's and China's influential nexus."

—Catherine Osborn, *Journalist and Foreign Policy columnist*

"From building airports to engaging in the Amazon forest, China has strengthened its foothold in Brazil. How should we think about this relationship and its strategic implications? A comprehensive look at the Sino-Brazilian relationship and its zenith in the second decade of the 21st century. Dr. Santoro's thoughtful analysis in *Brazil-China relations in the 21st Century* provides the much needed local and global context for this significant but less-studied bilateral relationship."

—Dr. Vishakha N. Desai, *Chair of Committee on Global Thought, Columbia University and President emerita, Asia Society*

CONTENTS

LIST OF TABLES

CHAPTER 1

The Sino-Brazilian Strategic Partnership: In Search of a Multipolar World

The history of the bilateral relationship between Brazil and the People's Republic of China began with an unlikely dialogue between the administrations of a Brazilian anticommunist general and Mao Zedong. It was a conversation driven less by their individual traits and preferences, and more by the winds of change which were blowing through the Cold War in the 1970s, transforming international order and opening diplomatic perspectives for Global South countries.

This initial chapter analyzes how Brazil and China developed their strategic partnership. The first section deals with the Brazilian decision to recognize the People's Republic in the 1970s and how Brasília and Beijing saw each other as a partner in terms of a possible Global South dialogue in search of a multipolar order.

The second section addresses the beginning of a deeper relationship in the 1980s, with the start of bilateral high-level visits and the creation of an innovative joint program to build satellites. The text discusses how Brazilian and Chinese leaders perceive each other and what they were looking for in the relationship, in a context of deep economic changes in both countries—the reform and opening in China and the foreign debt crisis in Brazil.

Following that, the third section studies the negotiation of the strategic partnership in 1993—at the time, a tool that neither country had used in

© The Author(s), under exclusive license to Springer Nature Singapore Pte Ltd. 2022
M. Santoro, *Brazil–China Relations in the 21st Century*,
https://doi.org/10.1007/978-981-19-0353-3_1

its diplomatic relations. The text argues that it was an unusual and somewhat rhetoric solution to problems that arose from political instability and a trade exchange that was often below expectations.

The last section of the chapters analyzes the late 1990s, a period where Brazil and China were "distant allies," in the words of former Brazilian president Fernando Henrique Cardoso. Despite the strategic partnership, there were many unmet expectations concerning trade and investments, although both governments were searching for ways to improve the relationship, that they saw as something with great potential—possibilities that would be achieved later, in the global commodity boom of the early twenty-first century.

1.1   The Brazilian Decision to Recognize the People's Republic of China

Brazil recognized the PRC in 1974, in the beginning of general Ernesto Geisel tenure as the Brazilian president (1974–1979). Military officers had been ruling the country as a dictatorship since the 1964 coup d'État and would remain in power for more 11 years. The authoritarian regime was anticommunist and had fought and destroyed armed groups of the Marxist left, including attempts of creating rural guerrillas supported by the Chinese. The Brazilian communists were affected by Sino-Soviet split, with factions organized according to their alliances towards Beijing or Moscow (Brands 2010; Gorender 1987; Hershberg 2021).

Geisel was a key player in the dictatorship from the beginning and defended the political repression. But he was also a pragmatic technocrat who understood that the regime needed to change and that the military could not stay in office forever. He initiated domestic reforms towards what he called a "long, gradual and safe" political opening. In his foreign policy, he decided to explore possibilities of dialogue and trade with Africa, Middle East and China. Brazil was facing a difficult economic moment, with rising international interest rates, growing foreign debt and the need to import large amounts of oil and to increase its exports (Cervo and Bueno 2002; Spektor 2010; Visentini 2004).

The Brazilian dictator was not alone in his desire to establish relations with China. Since the early 1970s, the American President Richard Nixon and his top foreign policy advisor Henry Kissinger were working on a diplomatic rapprochement between Washington and Beijing, with the aim to join forces against the Soviet Union and to end the war in Vietnam.

This groundbreaking geopolitical shift opened the way for many countries in Latin America to do something similar, although for different reasons.

The Latin American governments searched for more autonomy in their international relations, trying to diversify their political and economic partners among the communist countries and the new Third World nations born out of decolonization. Argentina, Brazil, México and Venezuela attempted at least some degree of this kind of diplomatic movement in the 1970s (Brands 2010). These countries, together with other major Latin American nations such as Colombia and Perú, would recognize China along the decade. It was a sharp contrast with the beginning of the period, when communist Cuba and socialist Chile were the only countries in the regions which maintained relations with Beijing (Becard 2008, p. 63).

Brazil stood out in this group because at the time it was the only right-wing military dictatorship. General Geisel and his minister of Foreign Affairs, ambassador Antônio Azeredo da Silveira, had to persuade the hardliners in the government that it was a good idea to recognize the PRC. The regime was indeed searching for more autonomous relations with the United States, because of conflicts with Washington regarding human rights violations and its nuclear program. But the Armed Forces were cautious about engagement in what they perceived to be anti-Western initiatives, such as the Non-Aligned Movement, and hostile towards communist regimes.

Geisel and Silveira motivations for recognize China were political; they thought that Sino-Brazilian dialogue would enhance Brasília's position in international organizations, where they shared with Beijing a high number of convergent opinions. Despite the differences in their political systems, both countries were developing nations with a critical approach to Global North States and in search of more autonomy. They understood that their best interest was a multipolar international order, and this guideline would be important for many other negotiations among them. To recognize, the PRC would enhance Brazil's international stand in Western Europe, in Africa and in Asia, said Minister Silveira (Spektor 2010, p.106).

However, there was not a consensus in the Brazilian government about the People's Republic of China. The president and the minister of Foreign Affairs had to persuade the Armed Forces, in a debate that mostly took place in Brazil's National Security Council. In order to convince the military officers, Silveira presented reestablishing ties between Brasília and Beijing less in terms of political goals and more about exploiting economic opportunities and creating markets for Brazilian exports: "We had to highlight the economic issue just to make the recognition palatable. But the problem was exclusively political. Economics would come with time, in a much broader timetable" (Quoted in Spektor 2010, p. 108).

This approach worked, in the context of rising concerns in the regime about the viability of maintaining high levels of growth for Brazil and keep its balance of trade. However, it was not unanimous: there were 17 votes in favor at the National Security Council, but five against recognize China, including the powerful minister of the Army, general Sylvio Frota. The Navy's chief of staff also opposed the movement, saying that it was "inconvenient to establish relations with the PRC" and that the rapprochement did not present "any advantage to National Security" (Quoted in Becard 2008, p. 68).

Silveira's movement played with Brazilian leader's older expectations about China. In the early 1960s, still in the democratic regime, there was a debate about the opportunities of trade with the PRC, and even a visit of the then vice-president João Goulart to the Asian country.

At the time—1960–1964—Brazil was in political turmoil, with rising left-wing movements and an attempt of several governments to implement a more autonomous foreign policy after the Cuban Revolution and strong nationalistic debates. As ambassador João Augusto de Araújo Castro, minister of Foreign Affairs said in his speech at the 1963 opening of the United Nations General Assembly, international politics was not just about East and West (the Cold War) but also about North and South (development): "Not everything is East or West in the United Nations in 1963. The world has other cardinal points. These terms, that until a little time ago dominate all international politics, could eventually be turned back to geography" (Quoted in Corrêa 2007, p. 172).

Many Brazilian diplomats and political leaders saw the People's Republic as a partner with great potential for this kind of diplomatic dialogue. However, there was an ideological split between left and right, among the polarization taking place in Brazil's domestic policy at the time. The coup d'État of 1964 interrupted this rapprochement with Beijing and turned the subject into a taboo for a decade.

Actually, one the first actions of the authoritarian regime was to arrest nine Chinese officials in Brazil, from a trade mission and from the Xinhua News Agency. The authorities charged and convicted them of espionage, but they were released in the next year after an international campaign and the work of Brazilian famous human rights champion, lawyer Heráclito Sobral Pinto (Shen 2020b).

The dictatorship saw Beijing through Cold War lens, but the generals sent a few trade missions to analyze the economic scenario. There was also the initiative of business leaders, such as Horácio Coimbra, the CEO of Café Solúvel, major coffee-export company. Coimbra traveled to China in the 1970s in several occasions, visiting the trade fair in Guangzhou, and became an enthusiast of the potential of the Chinese market for Brazilian agricultural products such as coffee, cotton and sugar. He was an influential and respected figure in the establishment of the military regime.

From the perspective of the PRC, the Chinese political and diplomatic leadership received Brazil's request with enthusiasm, in the remembrance of veteran diplomat Chen Duqqing. Among his peers working with Latin American issues in the Ministry of Foreign Affairs, the relationship with Brazil was seen as "natural alliance" (Biato Junior 2010, p. 40). In this evaluation, there were perceptions of the size and international influence of both nations, and of their role in their respective regions, but also of their similar positions concerning the global order due to the fact that they defended the multilateral system and the United Nations and feared an American hegemony of world politics, favoring a multipolar order of independent poles of power in Europa, Asia and Latin America (Biato Junior 2010, pp. 36–37).

The Chinese diplomats and politicians understood that anticommunism was a serious issue in Brazil and tried to ensure their Brazilian colleagues that Beijing had moved away from its geopolitical project of exporting revolution, and in the mid-1970s was searching for pragmatic ties that did not depend on ideological convergence, and committed to the Five Principles of Peaceful Coexistence, which include mutual non-interference in internal affairs (Wen 2004).

This message was delivered by vice-minister of Foreign Trade Chen Chieh, the top Chinese authority to visit Brazil during the negotiations for the diplomatic recognition, who highlighted the five principles of peaceful coexistence defended by Beijing, that is: mutual respect to sovereignty and territorial integrity; mutual non-aggression; non-intervention in the internal affairs of a country by other nation; equality; and reciprocal benefits. In that context, he presented proposals to improve bilateral trade (Becard 2008, p. 70).

During the first years of the bilateral relationship, Sino-Brazilian exchanges would remain small and discreet. Both governments opened embassies in their capitals, but that was all. The Chinese wanted to create a consulate in São Paulo to boost economic ties, but the Brazilians refused. Trade was just US$19 million in 1974 and US$200 million in 1979. A limited amount which reflected the situation of what was then two closed economies, with little engagement with each other (Becard 2008, pp. 72–75).

1.2   THE 1980S: THE START OF HIGH-LEVEL VISITS AND THE COOPERATION IN SPACE TECHNOLOGY

The relationship started to change and to become something more meaningful in the 1980s, due to major political and economic transformation happening in both countries, which created opportunities for an international rapprochement between them.

The long process of political opening in Brazil continued under Geisel's successor, general João Figueiredo (1979–1985). He was the last ruler of the military dictatorship, its final years marked by economic crisis, with foreign debt problems and high inflation. In his diplomacy, Figueiredo expanded Brazil's presence in the Third World, rebuilding partnerships with Brazilian neighbors and trying to expand markets for the country's exports. In that context, he also looked to the PRC as an opportunity.

In China, Mao Zedong died in 1976, and after political conflicts, the reformist faction of the Communist Party, led by Deng Xiaoping, was in power. In 1978, he began the opening and reform process to modernize the Chinese economy. China's leaders perceived Brazil as an important partner in South-South cooperation, with important lessons in development policy, science and technology, which could be useful to Beijing's goals.

The Figueiredo administration marked the beginning of high-level visits between China and Brazil's officials. His minister of Foreign Affairs, ambassador Ramiro Saraiva Guerreiro, became the first head of his ministry to visit China, in 1982. He met Deng Xiaoping and discussed trade, scientific cooperation and the Chinese reforms (Guerreiro 1992, p p. 169–171). The president himself followed him, in 1984, in the company of 100 businesspeople interested in trade with the Chinese, to mark the ten-year anniversary of the diplomatic ties.

The PRC that they met was a very different country than the one that had established diplomatic relations with Brazil, just one decade before, when China was emersed in Mao Zedong's Cultural Revolution, with an economy closed to the world. However, Beijing was still a city of low-rise buildings, with at most five floors, without elevators. The capital expanded just to the third ring road, instead of the seven that exist in 2021. Most people moved around in bicycles. There were no shopping malls and just a few international hotels, which often served as well as the headquarters of Chinese state-owned companies. The most important link to the outside world was a small airport, with two terminals. The diplomatic community lived in isolated compounds and had its own stores to buy products from the global market. The income per capita was just US$300 per year (Abdenur 2019; Gokhale 2021; Tang 2021).

Chinese diplomat Gao Kexiang, who served three times in Brazil, saw Figueiredo's visit as a watershed, when the Brazilian political leaders ceased to perceive China as an ideological problem and started to see it more as other developing country with shared interests: "We left behind the past of lack of confidence, we turned the page. Before that visit, we had been tried in vain to broad the relations beyond trade" (Quoted in Biato Junior 2010, p. 44). He compared that moment with the more difficult scenario of the mid-1970s, when the political differences and the mistrust were still big and make it difficult to establish a close partnership. Gao liked to quote Brazil's former minister of Foreign Affairs, Azeredo da Silveira, who told him that the Brazil-China relation is like an elephant: walks slowly forward, sometimes stop and after that finds its way back, but hardly moves backward (Quoted in Biato Junior 2010, p. 46).

At that point, Brazil was an important inspiration for China's own development projects, with more advanced technology in several key areas. Chinese officials started to visit the Latin American nation to learn from experiences such as the Itaipu hydropower dam—then, the biggest of the world—and the special economic zone of Manaus, in the Amazon, with its incentives for the installation of factories. Many years later, the CEO in Brazil of State Grid, China's giant state-owned enterprise would summarize how important these exchanges were to him and his colleagues. He said that in the 1980s Brazil was "a paradise of technologies that the Chinese colleagues desired," due to the construction of the Itaipu Hydropower dam and technologies such as the hybrid energy network. He considered "Brazilian colleagues were not only worth of our respect, they were also our teachers" (Cai 2020, p. 106).

Although bilateral trade was still very small and investment inexistent, Brazil and China were discovering that they could cooperate with each other to promote development. They were both Global South countries facing huge economic challenges, trying to keep some level of autonomy from the West and to learn from each other. These issues were highlighted by Deng Xiaoping himself, in his talks with Figueiredo, when he noticed that the Brazilian experience was about political opening and quick development. But he also warned that "Your lesson is to be in excessive debt. We will absorb your experience of quick development, but we will learn from you and avoid excessive debt" (Quoted in Shen 2020a, p. 30).

Deng and Figueiredo bonded personally through their common experience in the military, and the Brazilian president was sympathetic to what he saw, although later in life he would be dismissive of China, considering the country to be too poor and backward (Pasqualette, 2020). However, the visit was a watershed and it opened way to more dialogues and initiatives.

When foreign minister Saraiva visited China, he signed the first bilateral agreement on scientific cooperation. In 1985, the dictatorship ended in Brazil and the country returned to civilian rule, under president José Sarney (1985–1990), a conservative politician. He chose as minister of Science his party colleague Renato Archer, a former diplomat and navy officer, who had a great interest in international affairs, unusual among his peers. His chief diplomatic advisor was Celso Amorim, who later would be a very influential ambassador and minister. The following year, Archer visited China and identified possibilities for scientific cooperation. It was an unusual combination of high-level officials interested in improving Sino-Brazilian ties (Câmara 2021).

Brazil and China had created their space programs in the 1950/1960s, as part of an effort to promote scientific and technological development and achieve the mastery of high-level skills that were usually exclusive of great powers, and not developing nations. However, they were both facing troubles. Brazilians were in the middle of a deep financial crisis, with few resources to dedicate to science. The Chinese were beginning their opening and reform process, dealing with concern from the Global North about their research projects that had military uses, such as the space program (Chang 1996; Cunha 2004).

Archer's visit led to a dialogue at the technical level between the staff of Brazil's National Institute of Space Research (INPE, in the Portuguese acronym) and the Chinese Academy of Space Technology (CAST). For the next couple of years, they developed a proposal for a joint-venture to build and launch a satellite.

The initiative came from the Chinese. Their space program was built based on triad of satellites, rockets and the development of nuclear weapons. As such, it faced many restrictions from the West. However, Brazil did not have these problems. Brazilian scientists and engineers had often trained abroad and completed internships at NASA or Europeans institutions, and were familiar with state-of-the-art technologies and procedures. China's science officials understood that they could learn from the Brazilians. They sent many scientists to work at INPE, and in due time, several of them, such as Yuan Jiajun and Ma Xinrui, would build impressive careers as officials, including leadership positions in ministries, provincial governments and the central committee of the Communist Party (Câmara 2021).

Brazil's perspective was different. The country becoming a democracy again, with great ambitions in filling the social gaps of the authoritarian regime and addressing problems such as poverty, inequality and low quality of public health. It also inherited from the dictatorship an ambitious foreign policy, which tried to establish itself as a middle-power, a leader among the Third World, and to control key advanced technologies, like the nuclear and space programs (Cervo and Bueno 2002; Visentini 2004). This is the political context that explains the Sino-Brazilian negotiations about space technology.

The program was called China-Brazil Earth Resource Satellite (CBERS) and it was, at the time, the biggest South-South international cooperation initiative in science and technology. CBERS was a watershed in the bilateral relations, pushing Brasília and Beijing to a much higher level of dialogue and opening the way to the establishment of a strategic partnership. It still exists today: the original goal of launching one satellite was expanded, and by 2021, six artifacts had been completed. However, it was a long and winding road, full of hesitations and setbacks.

After the first rounds of negotiations between the scientists at INPE and CAST, both countries agreed that they would build a satellite and that the costs would be divided in the following manner: 70% to China and 30% to Brazil. The budget was estimated in US$150 million, which

would prove to be an understatement, with difficult political consequences at a time of economic crisis in Brazil. Although the amount
may not sound much, the program was often underfunded due to
disputes between civilian, military officers for scarce resources for the
space program.

The CBERS agreement was signed in 1988, when president Sarney
visited China. The trip was successful and included moments of high
symbolism, such as the meeting between the Brazilian president and
Chinese leader Deng Xiaoping, who told him: "As well as cannot be
a Pacific Century without China, cannot be a Latin American Century
without Brazil" (Biato Junior 2010, p. 5). For Brazilian diplomat and
author Oswaldo Biato Junior, this was a key statement in the history of the
bilateral relationship synthetizing that the Chinese saw Brazil, a country
regionally important and, like China, has prepared to take a leading role
in the international scene of the twenty-first century in the face of veiled
opposition from the United States to this desire (Biato Junior 2010,
p. 36).

With the return to civilian rule in Brazil and the start of economic
reforms in China, anticommunism did not play the same role in the bilateral relationship that in the 1970s. High-level exchanges and a more
sophisticated political dialogue became the norm. But there was still
concern among the Armed Forces, which remained wary of deep cooperation with their Chinese peers. The partnership between INPE and CAST
to make a satellite did not extend to technologies that could have military
applications, such as a rocket-launching vehicle, although that possibility
was discussed (Cunha 2004).

However, at the same time, Brazil was dealing with the foreign debt
crisis and in an economic situation so bad that the 1980s would be
remembered in the country as "the lost decade." That meant that the
Brazilian government often did not have the money to implement the
CBERS.

1.3   NEGOTIATING THE STRATEGIC PARTNERSHIP

Roberto Abdenur was already a veteran of Brazilian foreign service when
he arrived in Beijing in 1988 as ambassador, with the priority to make
CBERS happen. The problem: he did not have any financial resources
to do that and had to work with the only tool at his disposal: "saliva,"
he said (Abdenur 2017). With a small staff at the embassy, he had to

persuade the Chinese that Brazil was serious about the cooperation, even if it not had the money to fulfill its obligations under CBERS. The way that he would solve this dilemma would open the way to create a formal "strategic partnership" among both countries.

By the late 1980s, China's economic development already had global impacts and bilateral trade with Brazil was booming, especially because of oil. The Brazilian state-owned enterprise Petrobras became the first foreign company to join Chinese efforts to exploit offshore reserves. Oil was Brazil's biggest import product from China—at the time, the Asian country was still a net exporter of hydrocarbon. In exchange, the South American nation sold goods from the steel industry.

The Sino-Brazilian trade reached US$1 billion by the end of the 1980s. China was Brazil's second biggest partner in Asia, only behind Japan. For the Chinese, Brazilian were the largest market in Latin America, about half of the trade with the region. However, these economic patterns were unstable, due to the huge debt crisis that Brazil was facing, with severe recession and hyperinflation. There were ups and downs in the bilateral trade, and in the early 1990s, there were years when Brazilian exports to Taiwan and South Korea overcame sells to the People's Republic (Biato Junior 2010, p. 63).

In the political arena, Brazil was consolidating its new democracy, although in an unstable economic scenario that let politicians and diplomats very sensitive to short-term pressures, such as the electoral cycle. In 1989, the country held its first presidential elections in almost 30 years, choosing Fernando Collor, a young governor from the small state of Alagoas in the Northeast, who promised to end inflation and fight corruption. He would fail in both tasks, suffering an impeachment in 1992, and replaced by his vice-president Itamar Franco (1992–1995).

In Beijing, ambassador Abdenur had to deal with the consequences of Brazilian political instability, reporting to three presidents and five ministers of Foreign Affairs during his four years' tenure. President Itamar Franco, for example, canceled a trip to China due to political problems in Brazil, to the great disappointment of the Chinese authorities, who pointed that six of the seven members of the Standing Committee of the Politburo—the apex of power in the Communist Party—had visited Brazil in the previous years (Spitzcovsky 2021). This kind of episode happened often with the president, who did not like to travel abroad and often used domestic crises as an excuse to cancel international trips (Amorim 2021).

And of course, Abdenur had to deal with China's own challenges, such as the 1989 Tiananmen protests. The demonstrations happened during Brazil's presidential elections and did not have much impact in the country's foreign or domestic politics—Brazilians were just too concerned with their own troubles. The small national community in Beijing, mostly students and diplomatic families, was evacuated, among fears of civil war in the PRC (Abdenur 2019). But Brasília did not join the West in imposing sanctions to China. On the contrary, Brazilian diplomacy refused to criticize in the public the Chinese government, considering the protests to be an internal affair.

The leadership of both countries was way beyond the ideological suspicions of the beginning of their bilateral relationship. In the early 1990s, they looked to each other as important partners in a time of political and economic hardship. Most of their diplomatic problems came from tensions with developed nations, and Beijing and Brasília saw South-South cooperation as tool to face these challenges.

The Chinese leadership was also facing its own post-Tiananmen reckoning, with the purge of former secretary-general of the Communist Party, Zhao Zyiang. Deng Xiaoping was negotiating a coalition to support the reforms, exemplified in his famous Southern Tour. The role that Chinese foreign policy played in these efforts was to be a tool for development, helping the country to obtain investments, technology and markets useful to the Four Modernizations that Deng was implementing.

The cycle of high-level visits and technical delegations continued despite the fall in the bilateral trade. In 1990, president Yang Shangkung visited Brazil. In 1992, it was prime minister Li Peng. In that year, Brazil hosted in Rio de Janeiro the United Nations Conference on Environment and Development, which also helped to establish Brazilian diplomacy as a political actor of global standing in important issues of the international agenda.

Among Brazilian and Chinese diplomats, it was gaining strength the idea that both countries needed some kind of political gesture to signalize that the bilateral relationship was important beyond the current economic problems. The solution came during a trip of vice-prime minister Zhu Ronji to Brazil.

He visited the usual spotlights that Brazil liked to show to Chinese authorities: the Manaus special development zone, the Carajás mining complex and the Itaipu dam. Ambassador Abdenur accompanied him and during an airplane trip from Foz do Iguaçu to São Paulo suggested the term "strategic partnership" to describe Sino-Brazilian relations. Zhu approved the expression and started to use it in his speeches, first to businessmen in the São Paulo Industry Federation (Fiesp) and then to the interim minister of Foreign Affairs Luiz Fernando Lampreia and president Itamar Franco in Brasília. The idea was well received by all audiences. In the words of Abdenur: "It is interesting to notice that the creation of certain 'concepts' and certain 'key ideas', are important to elevate the level of the bilateral relations, for they have a capacity of mobilization and persuasion" (Quoted in Biato Junior 2010, p. 67).

The concept was invented and consolidated in the diplomatic rhetoric of both countries between March and November of 1993, during three high-level visits of Chinese authorities to Brazil: minister of Foreign Relations Qian Qichen, Zhu Ronji and, finally, secretary-general and designated president Jiang Zemin.

Jiang trip to Brazil happened after the Bill Clinton administration refused him a visa to enter the United States, as part of series of political pressures related to Tiananmen. The Chinese leader responded going to Brazil and Cuba, to show to the Americans that China had diplomatic options in Latin America with countries that had autonomous foreign policy vis à vis Washington. Even so, the decision to use the expression "strategic partnership" towards the Brazilians caught the Chinese diplomats by surprise. For Jiang Yuande, China's ambassador to Brazil between 2002 and 2006, China was willing a rapprochement with Brazil due to the developmentalist experience that both countries shared, to the importance of the Latin American nation and because of its good economic perspectives. But the Chinese did not know how to implement that partnership, which they saw as something more of a long-run goal (Biato Junior 2010, p. 71).

The Strategic Partnership is, indeed, a vague term and it still challenges political analysts to this day, with a long debate about its meaning and eventual overstretch (Lessa 2010; Oliveira 2004, 2010; Feng and Huang 2014). It was the first time that both countries defined a relationship in that way. It is not a formal treaty, binding them to obligations.

It usually implies that the Sino-Brazilian relationship is important in multiple levels: trade, political dialogue, scientific and technological cooperation, etc. It also points to the hope that it has a future potential which will lead it to overcome the troubles facing it at the moment. In that sense, its own vagueness is an advantage, in the sense that it can be used by both governments in different ways, depending on the circumstances.

Actually, Brazil and China liked it so much that they would expand their strategic partnerships in the 1990s and 2000s to other countries and organizations, such as Russia, the European Union and many Latin American nations.

1.4   Distant Allies: The Unmet Expectations of the 1990s

Despite the expectations, the partnership was not something that had an immediate effect. The second half of the 1990s were a time of unmet expectations in trade and investment, and of slowly building of the CBERS project.

Jaime Spitzcovsky arrived in Beijing in 1994 to the correspondent of Folha de São Paulo, Brazil's leading daily. At the time, there were only two Brazilian journalists covering China: he and Jaime Martins, in the Portuguese language section of China Radio International. Spitzcovsky had reported from Moscow the decline and fall of the Soviet Union, what he called "the last empire of the twentieth century" and proposed to the newspaper to tell the story of the "rise of the first empire of twenty-first century" (Spitzcovsky 2021).

"At the time there was a lot of uncertainty concerning the economic reforms, and concern about the health of Deng Xiaoping," said Spitzcovsky. "Brazilian politicians and businessmen were starting to travel to China, to look for opportunities." They did not know for sure what they wanted, but they were keen to explore the possibilities, sometimes making mistakes of judgment (Spitzcovsky 2021).

The biggest frustration for Brazilian companies interested in China was the failed attempt of the construction companies to establish themselves in the Asian country and take part in the huge infrastructure projects that were underway, especially the Three Gorges Dam. Given how the Itaipu dam was an important reference for the Chinese, Brazil's firms believed they had a good chance of winning similar contracts and they opened offices in China (Biato Junior 2010; Spitzcovsky 2021).

The construction companies had a successful history of internationalization since the 1970s when, supported by the military government, they expanded through Latin America, Africa and the Middle East. They were in search of alternatives for the decline of the development model of the authoritarian regime, looking for opportunities in oil-rich countries and careful to follow Brasília's geopolitical roadmap, approaching nations that were important in Brazilian foreign policy (Campos 2017; Gaspar 2020).

China in the 1990s fitted all these characteristics, but Brazil's construction companies overestimated Brasília's influence in Beijing and underestimated the nationalism of the Chinese authorities. To build a modern energy infrastructure was, indeed, a priority for the People's Republic. But instead of the big international projects that the Brazilians conducted in Angola, Iraq or Libya, they faced a market closed to foreigners. For China, these infrastructure initiatives were a matter of national security and the opportunity to build national champions such as State Grid and Three Gorges Company.

The Brazilian contribution would be small: consulting contracts with the major Chinese companies, but limited to an advisory role, without big profits or responsibilities. In a few years, Brazil's construction companies closed their offices in China and returned to South America (Biato Junior 2010; Spitzcovsky 2021).

Brazil's macroeconomic and political life stabilized after 1994, with the Real Plan, that was able to curb the hyperinflation. Then finance minister Fernando Henrique Cardoso was elected president twice and ruled the country from 1995 to 2003.

Cardoso was a sociologist of international reputation, one of the main names of the dependency theory of the 1960–1970s, which studied Latin American underdevelopment in light of its insertion in the global economy. During the dictatorship, he went to exile in Chile, United States and France, worked for the United Nations and taught at foreign universities. With the redemocratization of Brazil, he became a politician, being elected senator from the state of São Paulo. President Itamar Franco appointed him minister of Foreign Relations and minister of Finance.

Cardoso's foreign policy was based on the strategy of "autonomy through integration" (Cervo and Bueno 2002; Vigevani et al. 2003) in which Brazil was becoming part of several international regimes and organizations in search of rules-based global order that could balance the power of post-Cold War United States.

The Brazilian government broke the long-standing opposition of the military regime and joined human rights agreements and the Non-Proliferation Treaty. From the economic perspective, Cardoso diplomacy seeks to establish confidence and credibility to international investors, consolidating Brazil as a stable country.

As ambassador Luiz Felipe Lampreia, Cardoso's minister of Foreign Affairs wrote: "In foreign policy, our basic goal was to insert Brazil in the international mainstream, gradually moving us away from the Third World postures which had been formulated in the past and from the ambiguities originated in the military regime, created in the concept of Brazil as great power" (Lampreia 2010, p. 144).

What was China's place in Cardoso's foreign policy? Beijing remaining important in Brasília's worldview of a multipolar global order, as well as other developing powers, such as India and South Africa. However, it was a different perspective from the recent past. Brazil was in search of a rapprochement with the West and toning down the Third World rhetoric that had been an important part of its diplomacy in the 1970s–1980s.

In his eight years as president, Fernando Henrique Cardoso visited China only once. In his diaries, he is impressed by the economic growth that the Chinese achieved after the Deng Xiaoping reform and opening period, but also skeptic about how long it will take the country to reach the development level of the West. The president criticizes in his diary China's human rights situation but also states that Brazil should not do it in public, and that it would not follow the United States line on the subject.

Cardoso's reflection on his lunch with prime minister Li Peng noticed that China had economic interests in Latin America, especially minerals, and that food was also an interesting possibility. However, he wrote "The Chinese are seeing Brazil as a distant ally, and because of that, without problems" (Cardoso 2015, November 5–13, 1996).

Bilateral trade was growing—Brazil's exports to China doubled during Cardoso's tenure (Vigevani et al. 2003)—but both countries were still years behind the global commodities boom of the early twenty-first century. In his memoirs, Lampreia notes his concern with Chinese dumping and unfair trade practices, and how it caused problems to Brazilian textiles (Lampreia 2010, p. 291).

Brazil supported China's entrance in the World Trade Organization, a strategy that fit well in Cardoso and Lampreia foreign policy vision of a strong multilateral system to promote global rules. It would also be a tool to ensure Chinese compliance to demands about competition and labor rights.

As other Brazilian presidents before and after him, Cardoso could see how important China was to international politics, but felt unsure about how to engage with Beijing, recognizing his lack of expertise about the country, and of Asia in general: "We know [what to do] about Europe and the European Union, but what about Russia? And, beyond, China, India? Until what point they are strategic partners, as we say?" (Cardoso 2016, March 17–29, 1997).

Cardoso's observations are an important testimony of how difficult it was to implement the concept of the strategic partnership. Although the idea was conceived in the 1990s, it would take a decade for it to be put in practice. It would be a consequence of the global commodity boom, of the rising Chinese interest in Brazil's food and raw materials, and of a new Brazilian government with a diplomatic vision of highlighting relations between developing countries.

Despite the problems, the more favorable economic situation in Brazil in the second half of the 1990s helped to break the deadlock of international cooperation with China. The concept of the strategic partnership was in the minds of politicians and businessmen of both countries, stimulating them to look for opportunities of cooperation and economic exchange (Spitzcovsky 2021).

The CBERS program finally received the resources that it needed. In 1999, the first CBERS satellite was launched by both countries and became a symbol of their joint achievements. Brasília and Beijing also agreed on the expansion of the program, opening the way to the construction of the six satellites that have been built so far, until 2021.

Ambassador Abdenur was not serving in Beijing anymore, but he was invited to the launching. As he saw the rockets reaching the atmosphere, he described the moment as the most rewarding of his almost 50 years in the diplomatic career (Abdenur 2019).

References

Abdenur, Adriana. "Memórias da China. Uma brasileira conta como viveu, aos 14 anos, os protestos da Praça da Paz Celestial, em 1989". *Piauí*, Issue 155, agosto de 2019.

Abdenur, Roberto. "Percursos Diplomáticos—Embaixador Roberto Abdenur". *Lecture at the Instituto de Pesquisa em Relações Internacionais*, Brasília. October 13 2017. Available at: https://www.youtube.com/watch?v=sZTA1T G3LKc&t=6376s

Amorim, Celso. Interview to the author. October 30, 2021.

Becard, Danielly Ramos. *O Brasil e a República Popular da China: política externa comparada e relações bilaterais (1974–2004)*. Brasília: Funag, 2008.

Biato Junior, Oswaldo. *A Parceria Estratégica Sino-Brasileira: origens, evolução e perspectivas.* Brasília: Fundação Alexandre de Gusmão, 2010.

Brand, Hal. *Latin America's Cold War.* Cambridge: Harvard University Press, 2010.

Cai, Hongxian. Nove anos de trabalhos duros no Brasil: a história de crescimento da State Grid Corporation no Brasil. In: Zhou Zhiwei e Wu Changsheng (eds) *Histórias de Amizade entre China e Brasil.* Beijing: China International Press, 2020.

Câmara Gilberto. Interview to the author. June 14, 2021.

Campos, Pedro Henrique. *Estranhas catedrais: as empreiteiras brasileiras e a ditadura civil-militar, 1964–1988.* Niterói: Eduff, 2017.

Cardoso, Fernando Henrique. *Diários da Presidência. Volume 2, 1997–1998.* São Paulo: Companhia das Letras, 2016.

———. *Diários da Presidência. Volume 1, 1995–1996.* São Paulo: Companhia das Letras, 2015.

Cervo, Amado Luiz, Bueno, Clodoaldo. *História da Política Exterior do Brasil.* Brasília: Editora da UnB, 2002.

Chang, Iris. *Thread of the Silkworm.* New York: Basic Books, 1996.

Correa, Luiz Felipe de Seixas-Corrêa. *O Brasil nas Nações Unidas, 1946–2006.* Brasília: Funag, 2007.

Cunha, Lilian Fernandes da. *Em busca de um modelo de cooperação Sul-Sul—o caso da área espacial nas relações entre o Brasil e a República Popular da China (1980–2003).* UnB, 2004.

Feng, Zhongping and Huang, Jing. China's Strategic Partnership Diplomacy: Engaging with a Changing World, *European Strategic Partnerships Observatory,* Working Paper 8, June, 2014.

Gaspar, Malu. *A organização: A Odebrecht e o esquema de corrupção que chocou o mundo.* São Paulo: Companhia das Letras, 2020.

Guerreiro, Ramiro Saraiva. *Lembranças de um Empregado do Itamaraty.* São Paulo: Siciliano, 1992.

Gokhale, Vijay. *Tiananmen Square: the making of a protest.* Mumbai: Harper-Collins India, 2021.

Gorender, Jacob. *Combate nas Trevas: a esquerda brasileira, das ilusões perdidas à luta armada.* 1987.

Hershberg, James. "The Brazilian Far Left, Cuba and the Sino-Soviet Split, 1963: New International Evidence on a Discordant 'Struggle for Ascendancy'". In: Tanya Harmer and Alberto Martin Alvarez (eds) *Toward a Global History of Latin America's Revolutionary Left.* Miami: University of Florida Press, 2021.

Lampreia, Luiz Felipe. *O Brasil e os Ventos do Mundo: memórias de cinco décadas na cena internacional.* Rio de Janeiro: Objetiva, 2010.

Lessa, Antonio Carlos. "Brazil's strategic partnerships: An assessment of the Lula era (2003–2010)". *Revista Brasileira de Política Internacional*, Volume 2, Issue 53, 2010.

Oliveira, Henrique Altemani de. "Brasil e China: uma nova aliança não escrita?" *Revista Brasileira de Política Internacional*, Volume 2, Issue 53, 2010.

———. "Brasil-China: trinta anos de uma parceria estratégica." *Revista Brasileira de Política Internacional*, Volume 47, Issue 1, 2004.

Paqualette, Bernardo Braga. *Me Esqueçam: Figueiredo, a biografia de uma presidência*. Rio de Janeiro: Record, 2020.

Shen, Yunao. "A história da visita do presidente Figueiredo à China." In: Zhou Zhiwei e Wu Changsheng (eds) *Histórias de Amizade entre China e Brasil*. Beijing: China International Press, 2020a.

———. "Advogado Pinto, que fez contribuições especiais à amizade entre Brasil e China." In: Zhou Zhiwei e Wu Changsheng (eds) *Histórias de Amizade entre China e Brasil*. Beijing: China International Press, 2020b.

Spitzcovsky, Jaime. Interview to the author. July 12, 2021.

Spektor, Matias. *Azeredo da Silveira: um depoimento*. Rio de Janeiro: Editora da Fundação Getúlio Vargas, 2010.

Tang, Charles. Interview to the author. September 10, 2021.

Vigevani, Tullo, OLIVEIRA, Marcelo e CINTRA, Rodrigo. "Política externa no período FHC: a busca de autonomia pela integração." *Revista Brasileira de Política Internacional*, Volume 15, Issue 2, 2003.

Visentini, Paulo. *A Política Externa do Regime Militar Brasileiro*. Porto Alegre: Editora da UFRGS, 2004.

Wen Jiabao. *Carrying Forward the Five Principles of Peaceful Coexistence in the Promotion of Peace and Development*. Beijing: Ministry of Foreign Affairs, 2004.

CHAPTER 2

The Global Commodities Boom and the Sino-Brazilian Trade

The Chinese port city of Guangzhou is renowned for its cuisine. One of its famous dishes is a soup with manioc and corn—two ingredients typical of Latin America. With a tradition of 2,500 years of maritime trade, Guangzhou's gastronomy is a living testimony of the centuries-old links between China and the region, which also extends to the widespread use of Latin American peppers in Asia and to Chinese objects found in archeological excavations in Mexico (Dott 2020; Kaplan 2021).

These old economic links experienced a huge boost in the early twenty-first century. The global commodity boom of the 2000s turned the PRC in the main commercial partner of Brazil, giving economic meaning to the strategic partnership negotiated in the 1990s. Trade between the two countries skyrocketed from US$3.2 billion in 2000 to US$100 billion in 2020 (see Tables 2.1 and 2.2). Chinese demand for raw materials, food and oil was so big that it changed Brazilian economy, helping to turning the South American nation in an agribusiness world power, but at the same time reinforcing fears of international dependence and deindustrialization in Brazil.

The dialogue between Brazil and the PRC began in the 1970s as an exercise in South-South cooperation, with ambitious joint-programs such as satellite construction and diplomatic visions of building a multipolar world. In the 2000s, the rise of the bilateral trade gave a more solid

M. Santoro, *Brazil–China Relations in the 21st Century*, https://doi.org/10.1007/978-981-19-0353-3_2

Table 2.1 Exports
from Brazil to China,
2000–2020

Year	Value in US$ billion
2000	1.08
2001	1.90
2002	2.51
2003	4.53
2004	5.43
2005	6.82
2006	8.39
2007	10.77
2008	16.51
2009	20.99
2010	30.74
2011	44.30
2012	41.22
2013	46.02
2014	40.61
2015	35.15
2016	35.13
2017	47.48
2018	63.92
2019	63.35
2020	67.77

Source Brazil's Ministry of Economy

ground to these goals, but it also changed the perspective of the relationship, which became increasingly an asymmetric partnership. China developed very fast, in contrast to the unstable Brazilian recent economic history, marked by recessions, crisis and low growth. In these few decades, Chinese development surpassed Brazil's in terms of income level and GDP size.

The result is that the bilateral trade consolidate itself as an exchange resembling a typical North/South pattern, in which China exports industrial products and Brazil, commodities. In the Brazilian case, since 2010 between 70 and 80% of its exports to the Chinese market are concentrated in soy, iron ore and oil (Rosito 2020, p. 97). This a long way from the expectations of the past, when Brasília and Beijing thought of each other as partners to overcome the limitations of developing countries. This trade structure generated tensions and different visions of China as an opportunity or threat among Brazilian interest groups.

Table 2.2 Imports from China to Brazil, 2000–2020

Year	Value in US$ billion
2000	1.21
2001	1.32
2002	1.54
2003	2.14
2004	3.70
2005	5.33
2006	7.97
2007	12.59
2008	20.03
2009	15.90
2010	25.59
2011	32.78
2012	34.24
2013	37.32
2014	37.34
2015	30.71
2016	23.34
2017	27.55
2018	35.15
2019	36.02
2020	34.77

Source Brazil's Ministry of Economy

Brazilian diplomat Luiz Augusto Castro Neves, a former ambassador to Beijing, likes to quote something that he heard from the ex-Chinese ambassador to Brasília Chen Duqing: "It is not Brazil who is selling to China. It is the Chinese who are buying from Brazil" (Castro Neves 2021). This is also reinforced by former Brazilian secretary of Foreign Trade, Welber Barral: "You don't sell commodities. Somebody buys them from you" (Barral 2021).

In other words, the growth of the bilateral trade is a consequence of the development and dynamism of the Asian partner, and not of the role played by the South American nation, which was more reactive, basically responding to global transformations. Analysts often complain about the lack of a Brazilian "grand strategy" to deal with the rise of China (Rosito 2020; Yang 2020) in contrast to the two white papers on Latin America that the Chinese government published in this century (China 2008, 2016).

This chapter analyzes the evolution of the Sino-Brazilian trade in the twenty-first century and its consequences for the bilateral relationship. It begins with an overview of what China is looking for in its relations with Latin America, discussing its search for raw materials, food, oil but also political support in multilateral organizations. It also analyzes how the United States is reacting to the rising Chinese presence in its traditional zone of influence.

The second section addresses the Sino-Brazilian trade, presenting the numbers, the general pattern of exchanges and the transformations since the establishment of the bilateral relations in 1974. It shows how trade went from Brazil selling steel products and buying oil from the huge sums and the different patterns of today.

After that discussion, the chapter analyzes two important sectors of the Brazilian economy and the impacts they receive from Chinese trade: how China's demand helped to boost Brazil's agribusiness, becoming its main client, but also how cheap competition from Asia was another big blow in the deindustrialization process in the Latin American country, reinforcing fears of decline and economic insecurity.

The last section argues that the strong commercial links were important to expand Sino-Brazilian cooperation in the multilateral arena, helping, for example, in the creation of the BRICS, BASIC and in the dialogues in the two G20s (the financial one and the WTO).

2.1   China and Latin America in the Twenty-First Century

China's approach towards Brazil is part of its larger view of Latin America. China became very important to the region's economy in the twenty-first century. In the last 20 years, bilateral trade grew tenfold and the Chinese have consolidated themselves as the biggest economic partner of Argentina, Brazil and Chile, and among the major ones of Colombia, Mexico, Peru and Venezuela, with a total sum of US$ 300 billion per year. In the 2010s, they rose as a relevant source of foreign direct investment, with a capital stock in the region of about US$ 105 billion, concentrated in agriculture, energy and mining (Dollar 2017; Evan Ellis 2014).

China's rising economic interests in Latin America began after its accession to the World Trade Organization in 2001, when the country became more integrated to the global economy. Its subsequent growth created a huge demand for Latin American commodities, which has helped boost the region's development for almost a decade (Gallagher and Porzecanski 2010; Wise 2020).

On the multilateral level, China is looking for regional support on its most important issues (Taiwan, Tibet), became a member of the Inter-American Development Bank and created a cooperation forum with the Community of Latin American and Caribbean States (CELAC, in the Portuguese and Spanish acronym).

In colonial times, in Latin America, there were significant exports of silver from Spanish America to China, where the metal was used to buy silk, tea and porcelain. The Portuguese colony of Macau was an important trade hub, and the Brazilian ports were also a part of the maritime route from Europe to Asia. In many ways, this was the first real global network of commerce, connecting Eurasia to the Americas (Gordon and Morales 2017).

In the nineteenth century, with the wars and rebellions in China, there was a flux of Chinese emigrants to the Americas, especially to Cuba, Mexico, Panama and Peru. In Brazil, the Portuguese king John VI invited a group of a few hundred Chinese farmers to settle and produce tea—which they did, but without commercial success due to the inferior quality of the product (Costa and Borba 2015; Goyano 2018).

Later, in the second half of the century, there was a big debate about using Chinese peasants as a replacement for black slaves in Brazil, but due to racism against Asians only a small stream of immigrants was accepted on this base. Brazilian elites favored white and European laborers and considered the Chinese inferior, harder to adapt to the local culture (Lee 2018).

In the twentieth century, war and revolution in China basically interrupted the economic links with Latin America. Some migration still happened, with a mix of reasons—political refugees and/or Chinese looking for better opportunities. Most of them became small businessmen and joined the middle class (Araujo 2014; Piza 2012).

The Chinese diaspora also plays a role in the current Sino Latino-American trade. Often established as small shop owners, they usually maintain their personal connections in China and use their family networks to import cheap products from the country—such as toys and electronic equipment—which they sell to local consumers. In Latin American cities such as Buenos Aires and São Paulo, the Chinese shops are located in popular commercial neighborhoods like Once and Rua Vinte e Cinco de Março. In the Paraguayan Ciudad del Este, they play the role of trade outposts to merchants from several countries of the region (Pinheiro-Machado 2017; Piza 2012).

After Mao's death and the rise of Deng Xiaoping, the accelerated development of China changed the country into a huge consumer of food, energy and raw goods produced in Latin America. In the 2010s, China bought 10% of the oil it consumed from the region, 1/3 of iron ore (Gallagher 2016, pp. 45–47) and Brazil alone represented 2/3 of Chinese soy imports by the end of the decade (Rosito 2020, p. 102).

The Chinese also wanted the Latin American support for their major strategic concerns, such as Taiwan and Tibet. About half of the 14 countries which recognize Taipei are in the region, but as trade with the People's Republic of China had increased, some of the former Taipei supporters turned their diplomatic ties to Beijing, such as Costa Rica, El Salvador, the Dominican Republic, Nicaragua and Panama (Kahn 2018).

Since 2008, China's Ministry of Foreign Affairs published two White Papers containing the guidelines of its diplomatic strategy towards Latin America. The documents highlight the importance of trade and investment, but go beyond that, establishing a dozen sectors of cooperation and partnership in public policies (China 2008, 2016). In education, for example, the Chinese government created 65 centers for the study of Latin America and expanded the teaching of Spanish and Portuguese (Thomaz 2017).

How to deal with China became one of the main issues in the foreign policy of the United States. Although there is a strong economic relationship between both countries, with a bilateral annual exchange of US$550 billion in goods, divergent interests led to increased tensions, in particular in the disputes for maritime limits in the South China Sea and in the trade war launched by Donald Trump's administration.

In the academic and political debate, there is criticism about Washington's troubles to adapt to the new scenario with China as a major leader in a revitalized Asia (Cole 2013; Hayton 2014; Kaplan 2014; McGregor 2017; Rachman 2016), and warning on the "Thucydides' trap" where the rise of a new great power leads to war due to the fear of the current hegemon, as in the struggles between Athens and Sparta narrated by the Greek historian (Allison 2017).

The center of the discussions is the conflict for influence in Asia Indo-Pacific—a geopolitical concept now in vogue in American policy circles

(Auslin 2020; Doyle and Rumley 2019; Medcalf 2020)—but the rivalry with China is also present in the reflections on the foreign policy towards Latin America (Evan Ellis 2014; Gallagher 2016; Roett and Paz 2008). For many analysts, the growth in the Chinese influence in the region in the last two decades had a negative impact in American national interests, and Washington has been negligent and without clear guidelines in its policy for the region, in contrast to the dynamic Chinese actions (Gallagher 2017; Hsiang 2018).

Beyond the rise of Sino-Latin American trade, Americans have been watching with concern the increased engagement of China with infrastructure and defense in the region: investments, selling of arms and lending to governments with hostile relations with the United States, such as Venezuela. In recent years, the American government vetoed acquisitions of Chinese companies in their country and worried about similar transactions in Latin America. The focus of these efforts has been the activities of Huawei in the implementation of the 5G Internet pattern (Woods and Maveda 2018; Stuenkel 2020).

The American government is putting pressure on Latin American nations to ban Huawei from investing in 5G in the region, threatening them to cut access to international development banks or to suspend aid and international cooperation projects, especially in the smaller nations in Central America. However, this is not an easy choice, for these nations are also vulnerable to Chinese menaces, such as the establishment of barriers against exports (Londoño 2019). Besides, Huawei is already present in the major countries of the region as a provider of telecommunications equipment in Brazil and of cell phones in Mexico.

Especially under Trump, American diplomacy with Latin America has been concentrated in problems such as curbing migrations and organized crime. There is not a positive agenda for the region, such as trade deals. The American decision of quit the Transpacific Partnership was bad for countries such as Chile, Mexico and Perú, which considered the agreement a good way to boost their exports. The rise of protectionism and the revision of treaties such as Nafta contributed to feelings of anxiety and instability.

The Trump administration's most serious attempt to court Latin America away from China's influence was the initiative "Growth in the Americas" in 2019. The program aims to increase private investment in the region, with cooperation regarding adjusting the regulatory framework and procurement policy of the countries in the area.[1] However, this program does not offer direct official investment from the American government, which is actually dealing with serious problems of underfinanced infrastructure in the United States itself.

On the other hand, China has offered Latin America the possibility of joining the Belt and Road Initiative, its giant global infrastructure project. In this new "geopolitics of connectivity" (Abdenur and Gonzalez 2018), 20 countries of the region are now part of the New Silk Road, most of them in Central America and the Caribbean, the exception being Chile. Brazilian authorities, for example, say they want Chinese investment but through their own policies, and reject what they see as the political burden of joining the Belt and Road (Santoro 2021).

However, there are efforts of American scholars and diplomats in rethinking their historical relations with China and Asia in general (Campbell 2016; Green 2017) and similar studies on Chinese actions in Latin America (Evan Ellis 2014; Gallagher 2016), which could lead in the future to changes in policy.

2.2   Trade Between Brazil and China During the Global Commodity Boom

Brazil and China started to develop a strategic partnership based upon political perspectives: they identified each other as major partners among Global South nations in joint efforts to influence the international order towards a multipolar system. However, there it was always difficult for authorities in both countries to implement this view, which in the 1990s was more a long-term perspective than a reality on the ground.

The first decades of the bilateral trade followed a pattern where Brazil basically exported steel products to China and imported oil from the Chinese. This exchange reached at his peak about US$1 billion per year. It was enough to make China Brazil's second biggest partner in Asia, after Japan, and to consolidate Brazil as China's major Latin American market (Biato Junior 2010; Mattos and Santoro 2020).

However, this amount of trade was just a small percentage of what were at the time two economies still quite closed. There were many efforts from

---

[1] Official site: https://www.state.gov/growth-in-the-americas/.

diplomats from both countries to try to increase the flux, stimulating this or that product, but none really took off, and the bilateral exchange was subjected to the ups and downs of the international economy, especially the impacts of the Brazilian recessions.

The creation of the Brazil-China Chamber of Commerce illustrates this point. Its founder was Charles Tang, a Chinese businessman who was born in a Shanghai industrial family, which emigrated to the United States after the Revolution of 1949. Tang went to Brazil as a financial executive and made a career in the country. When Deng Xiaoping began the reform and opening period, he started to travel to China and reconnected to his relatives, some of which rose to be high-rank officials in the Communist Party (Tang 2021).

Through his family, he met then vice-prime minister Wu Xueqian, who in 1986 asked him to found a Brazil-China Chamber of Commerce. His argument: all major powers had one with the South American nation, and the Chinese should do the same. Back to Brazil, he talked to several businesspeople and politicians, but in general they were not enthusiastic about the idea, saying that China was too far away, too culturally distant, and they associated it with Chinese small shop owners in Brazil. However, there are a few exceptions, such as Fernando Henrique Cardoso (future president of the Republic, then a senator) and the respected journalist Herbert Levy (Tang 2021).

In the global commodity boom of the 2000s, trade created the sinews of the strategic partnership, providing a strong economic base from which Brazil and China would also cooperate more on political issues, such as the creation of the BRICS and global negotiations concerning the economy or climate change. In this sense, Sino-Brazilian dialogues are in a different scale than the rest of the relationships that Beijing maintains with other countries in Latin America.

This led to the creation of a sophisticated framework for the bilateral relation, as two Brazilian diplomats noticed, the bilateral relationship started to have a robust political-diplomatic framework, consolidated in the High Level Sino-Brazilian Commission [Cosban, in the Portuguese acronym, created in 2004], which allows to address problems and points of interest of each side in practically all areas of the Brazil-China cooperation (Correa and Barbosa 2017, pp. 30–31).

Cosban was indeed a major step in organizing the strategic partnership, creating a framework for drafting plans and establishing the agenda for the cooperation. In the words of ambassador Castro Neves, it was a tool to "operationalize the concept of the strategic partnership." The commission is led, formally, by the vice-presidents of each country. But it met only five times in 15 years.[2] Diplomats usually complain that its proceedings are too slow and bureaucratic.

The most important change in Brazilian foreign trade in the twenty-first century is the rise of China as its biggest export market, a position consolidated in 2009, during the global financial crisis that hit hard the West. Brazil's sales to the Chinese skyrocket from US$1 billion (2000) to US$16.5 (2008) reaching US$67.7 (2020) (see Table 2.1).

During the coronavirus pandemic, China was buying 1/3 of all Brazilian exports. The United States, Brazil's second largest market, acquired less than 10%.[3]

Brazilian sales to China are concentrated in commodities, with soy, iron ore and oil representing the majority of exports. Meat (cattle and swine) and cellulose were also important.[4] It is a trade highly dominated by a few products.

Brazilian imports from China jumped from 1.2 billion (2000) to 34.7 billion (2020). Brazil has had a constant superavit with China, so it does not face the same kind of trade discussions that countries with huge deficits, such as the United States, have been engaged for years.

Brasília's fears towards Beijing go in a different direction: excessive dependence on China and commodities, negative impacts on deindustrialization and trade policy conflicts between agribusiness and industry. An analysis on the date of the Sino-Brazilian commerce helps to explain why there are concerns like these.

Brazilian imports from China are more diversified than its exports. They are not dominated by a few products and instead include a broad range of telecommunication equipment, electronic components, machines, medical products and other types of industrial goods.[5]

There is a negative contrast between the big importance that China represents to Brazil and the lack of knowledge that Brazilians have about their main trade partner, even in specialized circles such as universities

[2] https://www.gov.br/mre/pt-br/assuntos/relacoes-bilaterais/todos-os-paises/republica-popular-da-china. Access in June 2021.

[3] Data from Brazil's Ministry of Economy. http://comexstat.mdic.gov.br/. Access in June 2021.

[4] http://comexstat.mdic.gov.br/pt/comex-vis. Access in June 2021.

[5] http://comexstat.mdic.gov.br/pt/comex-vis.

and press. In government, the information gap often means the absence of a long-term perspective on how to deal with China. Chinese know what they want from Brazil, the opposite is not true. So far, there has not been a single Brazilian White Paper on China, or anything like that from Brazil's officials.

The exceptions to this pattern have come from civil society. For example, the Brazilian China Business Council published in 2020 the report "Bases para uma Estratégia de Longo Prazo do Brasil para a China" [Base for a Brazil's Long Term Strategy Towards China]. Written by the Brazilian diplomat Tatiana Rosito, it highlights the international context, the Sino-American conflicts and analyzes data about trade and investment, identifying potential areas for more cooperation. The same institution had published in 2008 the document "Agenda China," with similar contents, although less detailed.

Another gap is the lack of Brazilian consulates in China, outside the seashore cities. Brazil has consular representations only in Beijing, Shanghai, Guangzhou and Hong Kong, with a proposal to open one in Chengdu. However, there are many dynamic urban centers in the West, such as Chongqing, with huge economic growth and potential (Correa and Barbosa 2017).

Ambassador Ana Cândida Perez was consul-general of Brazil in Shanghai, between 2012 and 2017. She arrived in China after a long career in Europe and was fascinated by the Chinese port: "The most modern and well-run city I ever saw" (Perez 2021). Shanghai was also the Brazilian consulate which most emitted business visa—a powerful mark of the importance of the Sino-Brazilian trade.

Ambassador Perez highlighted that the consulates are especially relevant for Brazilian companies and citizens in China, due to the relatively lack of contact between the two societies, and to the juridical need of consular seals for Sino-Brazilian business transactions. Everything needs to pass through the consulate (Perez 2021).

The Brazilian consulates in China are also important to help business-people facing troubles with the Chinese legal system. The big companies usually hire local law firms or consultancies to support their work, but small and medium enterprises often do not have this kind of knowledge and may experience several problems because of their low familiarity with the PRC legal system (Perez 2021).

The lack of an adequate structure for promoting Brazil's exports is not limited to the small numbers of consulates. The country has as specialized government agency dedicated to the issue, Apex. However, most of its employees work in Brasília, and in China, Apex has just a small office in Beijing.

The debate on trade promotion is not so much on soy, iron ore and oil, which comprises almost 80% of Brazilian exports to China, but how to identify and support the growth of other products with potential in the Chinese market, but which need an extra boost. It is also a discussion of developing Brazil's image among the Chinese public, especially using the actions of big companies already present in the country (Rosito 2020, p. 108).

Brazilian officials with experience of China highlight the importance for Brazil's companies to understand its society, the national culture and to have a presence on the ground in Asia. Former secretary of Foreign Trade Tatiana Prazeres points that Brazilian companies undertake few studies of the Chinese market and lack of knowledge about daily issues which are important for consumers—for example, the special role of packaging in China or the high developed e-commerce practices (Prazeres 2021).

2.3   HOW CHINA HELPS TO DEVELOP BRAZIL'S AGRIBUSINESS SECTOR

Brazil was inserted in the global economy as the producer of agricultural and mining goods. Portugal stated its colonization in the sixteenth century to extract Brazilwood—Brazil's country name is itself a commodity. The national economic history is made of a succession of cycles such as sugar cane, gold, coffee and rubber, usually exported to the United States and to Europe.

The global commodity boom of the 2000s added more names and places to that equation: soybeans, meat, iron ore, oil and China. The base for that started well before Deng Xiaoping initiated its four modernizations in Beijing; they are related to Brazil's own economic transformations in the twentieth century, which built the foundations for the development of the country as an agribusiness powerhouse.

Between 1930 and 1980, Brazil had an economic model known as "national-developmentalism," where the state was the main promoter of growth, stimulating industrialization and building infrastructure. Industry was protected from foreign competition through high tariffs and administrative barriers (Abreu 2014; Bielschowsky 2004).

At the time, Brazil's main agricultural export was coffee, but the country was not considered to be an agribusiness giant. On the contrary, the lack of modern farming practices, deficient infrastructure and financial problems (such as low credit to agriculture) often meant low productivity. Increases in production were usually the result of the expansion of the frontier, of the cultivated land. By 1960, the country was a net importer of food (Klein and Luna 2020).

This situation started to change in the military dictatorship of 1964–1985, which had several policies aimed at the modernization of agriculture. The regime promoted the transformation of the sector, from a source of savings to fund industrialization to a major economic powerhouse in itself (Barros 2020, p. 85).

The military stimulated the expansion of the economic frontier to Brazil's Center West, the region that is now the most important agribusiness region of the country. The government gave incentives for farmers to buy cheap land and established programs for agricultural loans and policies to ensure minimum prices and to keep stocks, maintaining demand. It multiplied public credit to agriculture by four times in the 1970s, helping farmers to buy equipment, fertilizers and seeds, boosting an industrial complex to support them. The cultivated area almost doubled (Klein and Luna 2020).

It was not something that happened naturally, for the soil of the Center West is quite acid, and it was not good for agriculture. However, bioengineering through Brazilian Agricultural Research Corporation (Embrapa), Brazil's state-owned company which is a reference in the field, helps to transform it in a more fertile ground. Embrapa's technology helped to boost productivity for several crops, but the most important for Brazil agribusiness—and to the bilateral trade with China—was soy, which in a few decades became the biggest national export.

Soybeans were well developed in Asia for centuries and were first brought to Brazil by Japanese immigrants in the 1950s, as a wheat-associated crop. There were several public policies to support the farmers, including scientific research by universities and Embrapa, and during the military regime, the soybean production multiplied by seven in the 1960s and by then in the 1970s (Barros 2020, p. 87).

When China emerged in the 2000s with its global hunger for food, Brazil was well positioned to supply the Chinese market with soybeans. They are used in the Asian country especially as animal ration, to feed the swine herd that is so important to China's cuisine. It is the simplest version of soy, without the industrial process that one can find, for example, in soybean oil. China's tariff structure reflects that. Chinese market is quite open to the import of raw soy, but with higher rates for more industrialized types of the product (Escher and Wilkinson 2019, p. 664; Barral 2021).

There are several reasons that explain why China turned to Brazil as major supplier for food. The most important one is the changes in the Chinese diet. Due to economic development and to the rise of family income, the meat consumption rose by four times since the beginning of the reform and opening process, reaching the average of 61 kg per person in 2010. It is low compared to the United States (120 kg), but above the world average (42 kg) and similar to Brazil (73 kg) (Escher and Wilkinson 2019, pp. 662–663). Although China is a major food producer, it could only respond to new levels of demand with massive imports.

China's entrance in the World Trade Organization, in 2001, was also a watershed in the liberalization of its market. As in Table 2.1, from 2002 on Chinese imports from Brazil rose at high speed, without interruption. The effect on Brazil's agribusiness was deep, with higher prices boosting production and cultivated area. Soybean prices rose 232.84% between 2006 and 2012, and production grew 6.7% each year (Escher and Wilkinson 2019, p. 666).

China was a new challenge for Brazil's agribusiness. Until the 2000s, the majority of the exports of the sector went to the European Union. The production was also bought, mostly, by the giant Western trading companies—Archer Daniels, Bunge, Cargill and Louis Dreyfus—the so-called ABCD group. These were the traditional partners of Brazilian farmers.

The Chinese rise changed that, leading to a new "geopolitics of soy" (Oliveira 2015), with China consolidating itself as the destination of 2/3 of Brazilian exports of soybeans. The game changed in many ways. Not just in terms of new markets, but also about the traders, for the ABCD group lost ground in Brazil to Asia's agribusiness giant China Oil and Foodstuffs Corporation (COFCO), which became a global player during the commodity boom.

The Chinese government founded COFCO in 1949, but its internationalization began in the 2000s, as part of the "go global" strategy of China. It entered the Brazilian market through brownfield investments, buying assets from companies from Europe (Nidera) and Singapore (Noble). By the mid-2010s, COFCO and other Chinese firms such as Hunan Dakang were buying more Brazilian grains than the ABDC group (Escher and Wilkinson 2019, pp. 673–674).

Brazil's agribusiness adapted quickly to Chinese demands and it benefited a lot from the new markets in Asia. But it was never in charge of the relationship. China defined what to buy, the tariff levels, the international logistics of the operation and so on.

Nevertheless, the gains to the Brazilians were expressive and fundamental to consolidate the 2000s and the first half of the 2010s as a period of growth and good perspectives for agribusiness. By the end of the decade, the sector was responsible for 21% of Brazil's GDP and it played an important role in containing inflation and reducing poverty, from falling real prices (Barros 2020, pp. 72–73).

However, there are important qualifications to how Brazilian agribusiness profits from China. Soybeans are the big winners, but other important agricultural products failed to leave their mark in the Chinese market. Coffee is a good example. Its consumption has been growing 15% per year in China since 2010, and Brazil is the world's largest producer; it exports under US$25 million to the country, and its brands are not well known to local consumers, for it is usually bought as part of a blend in major coffee houses (Inova China 2021).

This an issue highlighted by former secretaries of Foreign Trade, who notice that although almost 20% of China's agriculture imports are from Brazil, there is not much perception among Chinese consumers of a "Brazilian brand" associated with the country and its products. In many cases, they even don't know that they are buying goods from Brazil (Barral 2021; Prazeres 2021).

This part of a bigger picture of structural problems of Brazilian foreign trade is discussed in this chapter: lack of adequate promotion, low initiative from firms and excessive dependence on external demand. Difficult to access the Chinese market is an extreme version of these challenges (Dutra and Wachholz 2021).

The huge dependence of Sino-Brazilian trade on commodities also stimulates two big debates. One is about the environmental impacts of the bilateral relationship—this will be the main issue of Chapter 4 of this book. The other discussion is if China has an impact on Brazil's deindustrialization process—the subject of the next section.

2.4   China and Brazil's Deindustrialization

The rise of China as the "factory of the world" led to fears of deindustrialization in many countries, due to the challenges of international competition with the Asian giant, among concerns about the low cost of Chinese labor, subsides, the quality of infrastructure and other factors. This debate has been quite strong in Brazil, where several economic trends since the 1980s had negative effect on industry, in contrast to the agribusiness boom.

In his seminal study on "premature deindustrialization," economist Dani Rodrik identified Latin America as the region more affected by that phenomenon. He argues that rich countries deindustrialized at a high level of income and made the transition to a sophisticated service economy. It is a different scenario in developing nations, which have imported deindustrialization from abroad, after the opening of their economies in the 1980s and 1990s (Rodrik 2016).

Other authors agree with Rodrik and point Chinese competition as a main threat to Latin America putting the region back into a world of primary product dependency, outperforming Latin America in global manufacturing markets. They estimate that up to 94% of the regional industrial production may be under negative impacts of China's rivalry (Gallagher and Porzecanski 2010).

There are also more moderate views on Chinese influence in Latin American industrial production. Carol Wise notice, for example, that Mexico did not experience any kind of reprimarization due to China's competition and that the reasons for the economic troubles of each country should be looked for in its policies, institutions and domestic situation, in how each nation responded to the changes in global competition (Wise 2020).

Brazil was perhaps an extreme view of these concerns, because of the central role that industry played in the 1930-1980s national-development cycle. The unifying project of presidents Getúlio Vargas (1930–1945; 1950–1954), Juscelino Kubitschek (1956–1960) and the military regime (1964–1985) was to modernize the Brazilian economy and turn the country into an industrial powerhouse (Bielschowsky 2004). This idea entered in crisis with the foreign debt crisis of 1982 and the "lost decade" for Latin America that followed it.

In his comprehensive review of the literature on Brazilian deindustrialization, Paulo Morceiro (2012) analyzes several authors who study the subject and he discusses indicators from different point of views, especially GDP and employment levels. His most important conclusion is that Brazil suffers from premature deindustrialization since the 1980s. Although there were moments of recovery (1999–2004), the trend is strong towards the decline of industry (Morceiro 2012, p.202).

The share of industry in Brazil's GDP fell from 36% in 1985 to 11% in 2011. For the first time since the 1950s, it is a smaller percentage than the sum of agriculture and cattle-raising (Morceiro 2021). However, there are important differences in terms of industrial sectors. Segments such as the automobile industry or transportation increased their output in an expressive way in that period. The negative impacts are concentrated in electronic and telecommunication equipment, apparel, wood products and shoes. There is an almost perfect correlation with Chinese imports (Morceiro 2012, p. 109).

Brazil's National Confederation of Industry organized a survey on how its associated view Chinese competition. Only 28% of the companies said that they compete with China in the Brazilian domestic market, and 13% stated that they are rivals abroad. There are important difference among the industrial sectors. In the domestic market, the ones which reported more concern about Chinese competition are textiles (61%), computers and electronics (61%), metallurgy (56%), apparel (51%), electrical machines (48%) and shoes (46%). Concerning disputes for foreign markets, the biggest percentages are shoes (30%), leather (20%) and textiles (20%) (Conferederação Nacional da Indústria 2015).

In its reports and lobby efforts, the National Confederacy of Industry complains about China's unfair trade practices, such as subsides, question its actions and demand responses from Brazil at the WTO or other forums. But it also defends the expansion of bilateral trade (Confederação Nacional da Indústria 2020).

There were moments when Brazilian industrial leaders were more protectionist and defended more trade barriers against Chinese competition. One of these episodes was the Lula administration's decision to recognize China as a market economy, in 2004. PRC's president Hu Jintao presented the request to Brazilian ambassador Castro Neves, in their first meeting (Castro Neves 2021). Although it was not implemented due to the opposition that it created, it provoked strong discussions inside the government and among business associations (Amorim 2021; Barral 2021).

The industrial leaders were concerned about the negative effects that the recognition would create to government actions against Chinese dumping and other commercial defense policies. Complaints about illegal practices from China's companies were a big part of the daily life of the secretary of Foreign Trade, but not all of them were well funded (Barral 2021). Inside the Lula's administration, the strongest opponent of recognizing China as a market economy was vice-president José Alencar, a textile industrial leader, with strong links to the sector more negatively affected by Chinese competition (Amorim 2021).

Another important moment of Brazilian industrial protectionist pressures against China was Dilma Rousseff's administration (2011–2016). In the evaluation of then secretary of Foreign Trade Tatiana Prazeres, it was a combination of concerns about "currency wars" and an overvalued Real with a more assertive industrial policy, with the State taking a bigger role in promoting Brazil's companies (Prazeres 2021).

For Prazeres, the concerns of Brazilian industrial firms had many reasons, and competition from China was just one of them. They also reflected structural problems, such as lack of international dynamism, difficulties to finance exports and logistical obstacles—and even a historical experience of high government protection during the national-developmentalist period and the challenges of adapting to a more open integration to the global economy (Castro Neves 2021; Prazeres 2021).

The troubles of Brazil's industry are real, but they fall back to the crisis of the national-development model of the 1980s and the challenge of adapting to a more open, integrated and competitive global economy. The rise of China and other Asian nations as industrial powers is just one more chapter in this history.

2.5   Beyond Trade: A Global South Partnership

The global commodities boom happened at the same time that the left-wing Workers' Party was ruling Brazil, under presidents Luiz Inácio Lula da Silva (2003–2010) and Dilma Rousseff (2010–2016). Their administrations implemented a foreign policy dedicated to the promotion of South-South dialogue and to the diversification of Brazilian diplomatic partnerships in Africa and Asia, in an effort to promote economic development, to reduce imbalances between Brazil and the great powers and to increase the influence of the country in international negotiations (Guilhon-Albuquerque 2014; Lessa 2010; Vigevani and Cepaluni 2007).

China was from the start of the Workers' Party administrations an important component of that strategy. Although Lula and other party leaders had stronger ties with the Latin American and European left, and knew little of China, their diplomatic teams at the Ministry of Foreign Affairs were veterans of the Sino-Brazilian relationship.

Ambassador Celso Amorim, who served as Lula's minister of Foreign Affairs for eight years, had been working with Beijing since the CBERS program in the 1980s and as Brazil's representative to the WTO also helped with the Chinese accession to the institution. In 1974, when the Brazilian government recognized the PRC, Amorim volunteered to serve in Beijing and to help in the opening of the embassy, but at the end he went to Brasília to work as top-level advisor at the ministry (Amorim 2021).

In the view of the specialists, the Sino-Brazilian partnership under the Workers' Party administrations was reframed around three issues: economic matters (trade and investment), multilateral cooperation and a stronger sense of Global South identity (Guilhon-Albuquerque 2014; Oliveira 2010; Vigevani and Cepaluni 2007). In many ways, this a return to the perspectives of the 1980s, after years of a more low-profile relationship.

The rapprochement between Brazil and China began in 2003, when Lula took office. In that year, Brazil and China were among the countries that created the G20 at the WTO, to fight against agricultural subsidies from rich nations and to join forces in the Doha Round. The creation of the G20 was important to reaffirm the commitment to South-South cooperation and to show that it was feasible (Amorim 2005).

Lula visited China as president twice, in 2004 and 2009. He also met Chinese president Hu Jintao in other occasions, a total of eight times in his administration (Guilhon-Albuquerque 2014). This constant exchange of high-level visits led to an improvement in the framework for managing the strategic partnership.

The first one was the creation of the High Level Sino-Brazilian Commission (Cosban, in the Portuguese acronym) in 2004. Led by the vice-presidents of both countries, it is the main mechanism for the bilateral dialogue, drafting a 10-year cooperation plan. Cosban was very active in its first decade, although it later became stagnated.

The second important development was the creation of the Brazil-China Business Council (CEBC in the Portuguese acronym), which became the main partner in the economic dialogue between companies and governments of both countries, "the private arm of the Sino-Brazilian relationship," in the definition of ambassador Castro Neves, who after his retirement from the foreign service became its chairman. The founding of CEBC was a consequence of Lula's first trip to China, when the president took with him a delegation of 200 hundred Brazilian businesspeople in search of opportunities in Asia. The visit was also a landmark in establishing offices in Beijing of Brazil's SOEs, such as Petrobras and Banco do Brasil (Lessa 2010; Scolese and Nossa 2006).

Another very important initiative of the period was the creation of the BRICS in 2006, combining Brazil, China, India, Russia and, later, South Africa. A comprehensive study of the group is outside the scope of this book, but it is worth to notice that the partnership is something that makes Brazil stand out from other Latin American nations in its relationship with China. None other has such a strong bond with Beijing.

The BRICS has been described as a group dedicated to a "weak reformism" in multilateral economic affairs (Stuenkel 2015), aiming at a more equal distribution of power and influence but without presenting a direct political or military challenge to the West. Even so, it is a mark of the 2000s, of a more assertive Brazil demanding a bigger share of international influence.

The term BRICS was created by Goldman Sachs executive Jim O'Neill, but ambassador Celso Amorim jokes that when they met, he told him: "You created the BRICS, but I made it" (Amorim 2021). In other words, the political dialogue between Brazil and other emerging powers was essential to implement the concept drafted by the investment banker.

In 2012, the Sino-Brazilian bilateral partnership was rechristened as "Global Strategic Dialogue," with the establishment of sectorial forums not just on bilateral issues, but also in broaden international affairs, such as the situation of Latin America, the Middle East, disarmament discussions and so on. It is a symbolic gesture "which opens the door to more substantial content" (Castro Neves 2021).

Cosban has the responsibility to implement the Global Strategic Dialogue, organizing meetings and drafting long-term planning, such as the Common Action Plan (Brazil 2015), with a roadmap of the bilateral cooperation for the period between 2015 and 2021, highlighting points like education, health and innovation.

The partnership between Brazil and China during the global commodity boon was never a dialogue among equals; it was always marked by the unbalance of power towards Beijing and by a deep asymmetric pattern of trade that has been a constant source of concern for Brazilian officials. With all the rhetoric of South-South cooperation, a Brazil that exports food, minerals and oil to China, and imports from it manufactured goods resembles much more a structure of North–South dependency.

This problem has been noticed in many reports and studies prepared by Brazilian business associations (CEBC 2008; CNI 2020; Rosito 2020), which often recommend a mix of policies do deal with the challenge: trade defense, sectorial agreements, more commercial promotion and more attention to the international brand of Brazil.

So far, these measures have not been enough to face the structural differences between both nations and the challenges that Brazil faces in its international competition, especially when related to industrial products.

In the mid-2010s, Brazil faced a succession of crisis, with the end of the boon, corruption scandals which weaken the major parties and the rise of a new right-wing political movement with a critical view of China. These issues will be debated in Chapter 5.

REFERENCES

Abdenur, Adriana, González Levaggi, Ariel. "Trans-Regional Cooperation in a Multipolar World: How Is the Belt and Road Initiative Relevant to Latin America?" *London School of Economics Global South Unit: Working Paper Series*. N. 1. 2018.

Abreu, Marcelo de Paiva (org). *A Ordem do Progresso: dois séculos de política econômica no Brasil*. São Paulo: Elsevier, 2014.

Allison, Graham. *Destined for War? Can America and China Escape Thucydides's Trap?* Boston: Houghton Mifflin Harcourt, 2017.

Amorim, Celso. "Política externa do governo Lula: os dois primeiros anos." *Análise de Conjuntura OPSA*, Volume 4, March, 2005.

Amorim, Celso. Interview to the author. October 30, 2021.

Araujo, Marcelo da Silva "Culturaacima da Bíblia? História, religião e sociabilidade entre chineses de igrejas evangélicas no Rio de Janeiro." Tese de doutorado em Antropologia, Universidade Federal Fluminense, 2014.

Auslin, Michael. *Asia's New Geopolitics: Essays on Reshaping the Indo-Pacific*. Stanford: Hoover Institution Press, 2020.

Barral, Welber. Interview to the author. July 23, 2021.

Barros, Geraldo Sant'Ana de Camargo. "The Brazilian Agri-Food Sector: An Overview." In: M. Jank et alli. *China-Brazil Partnership on Agriculture and Food Security*. Piracicaba: Universidade de São Paulo/ESALQ, 2020.

Biato Junior, Oswaldo. *A Parceria Estratégica Sino-Brasileira: origens, evolução e perspectivas.* Brasília: Fundação Alexandre de Gusmão, 2010.

Bielschowsky, Ricardo. *Pensamento econômico brasileiro, o ciclo ideológico do desenvolvimentismo (1930–1964).* Rio de Janeiro: Contraponto, 2004.

Brazil. Plano de Ação Conjunta entre o Governo da República Federativa do Brasil e o Governo da República Popular da China—2015–2021.

Campbell, Kurt. *The Pivot: The Future of American Statecraft in Asia.* Nova York: Twelve Books, 2016.

Castro Neves, Luiz Augusto. Interview to the author. December 28, 2021.

China. *China's Policy Paper on Latin America and the Caribbean.* Beijing: Ministry of Foreign Affairs, 2008.

———. *China's Policy Paper on Latin America and the Caribbean.* Beijing: Ministry of Foreign Affairs, 2016.

Cole, Bernard. *Asian Maritime Strategies: Navigating Troubled Waters.* Washington: Naval Institute Press, 2013.

Confederação Nacional da Indústria. *Sondagem Especial 62—China.* Brasília: CNI, 2015.

———. *Agenda para a China.* Brasília: CNI, 2020.

Conselho Empresarial Brasil China. *Agenda China.* Brasília: CEBC, 2008.

Costa, Cristiane and Borba, Cibele de. *China Made in Brasil: personagens, curiosidades e histórias sobre dois séculos de aproximação entre o Brasil e seu principal parceiro comercial.* Rio de Janeiro: Babilônia, 2015.

Correa, Germano, Barbosa, Pedro Henrique. "Uma Tentativa Brasileira de Entender o Funcionamento do Governo e do Setor Privado na China". In: P. H. Barbosa (ed) *Os Desafios e Oportunidades na Relação Brasil-Ásia na Perspectiva de Jovens Diplomatas.* Brasília: Funag, 2017.

Dollar, David. *China's Investment in Latin America.* Washington: Brookings Institution, 2017.

Doyle, Timothy and Rumley, Dennis. *The Rise and Return of the Indo-Pacific.* Oxford: Oxford University Press, 2019.

Dott, Brian. *The Chile Pepper in China: A Cultural Biography.* New York: Columbia University Press, 2020.

Dutra, Ligia and Wachholz, Larissa. "Café, paçoca e açaí no e-commerce da China." *Valor Econômico*, June 7, 2021.

Escher, Fabiano and Wilkinson, John. "Economia política do complexo Soja-Carne Brasil-China." *Revista de Economia e Sociologia Rural*, Volume 57, Issue 4, 2019.

Evan Ellis, Robert. *China on the Ground in Latin America: Challenges for the Chinese and Impacts on the Region.* Nova York: Palgrave Macmillan, 2014.

Gallagher, Kevin. *The China Triangle: Latin America's China Boom and the Fate of the Washington Consensus.* Nova York: Oxford University Press, 2016.

———. "China steps into the Latin American Void That Trump Has Left Behind". Foreign Policy, March 6, 2017.

Gallagher, Kevin and Porzecanski, Roberto. *The Dragon in the Room: China and the Future of Latin American Industrialization*. Stanford: Stanford University Press, 2010.

Green, Michael. *By More Than Providence: Grand Strategy and American Power in the Asia Pacific Since 1783*. Nova York: Columbia University Press, 2017.

Guilhon-Albuquerque, José-Augusto. "Brazil, China, US: A Triangular Relation?" *Revista Brasileira de Política Internacional*, n. 57. 2014.

Gordon, Peter and Morales, Juan José. *The Silver Way: China, Spanish America and the Birth of Globalization, 1565–1815*. Sydney: Penguin Australia, 2017.

Goyano, Jussara. "Do tea ao tech: a saga dos imigrantes chineses no Brasil". *China Hoje*, N. 20, 2018.

Hayton, Bill. *The South China Sea: The Struggle for Power in Asia*. New Haven: Yale University Press, 2014.

Hsiang, Antonio. "As America Withdraws from Latin America, China Steps in." *The Diplomat*, January 4, 2018.

Inova China. *O Mercado de Café na China*, 2021. Available at: https://inovac hina.com/conteudo/relatorios/mercado-cafe-china/.

Kahn, Carrie. "China lures Taiwan's Latin American allies". National Public Radio, October 13, 2018.

Kaplan, Robert. *Asia's Cauldron: The South China Sea and the End of a Stable Pacific*. Nova York: Random House, 2014.

Kaplan, Stephen. *Globalizing Patient Capital: The Political Economy of Chinese Finance in the Americas*. Cambridge: Cambridge University Press, 2021.

Klein, H. and Luna, F. *Alimentando o mundo: o surgimento da moderna economia agrícola no Brasil*. Rio de Janeiro: FGV, 2020.

Lee, Ana Paulina. *Mandarin Brazil: Race, Representation and Memory*. Stanford: Stanford University Press, 2018.

Lessa, Antônio Carlos. Brazil's Strategic Partnerships: An Assessment of the Lula Era (2003–2010). *Revista Brasileira de Política Internacional*, n. 53, 2010.

Londoño, Ernesto. "To Influence El Salvador, China Dangled Money. The US Made Threats." *New York Times*, September 21, 2019.

Mattos, Thiago e Santoro, Maurício. "Ásia: novas fronteiras do comércio exterior do Brasil." *Revista Brasileira de Comércio Exterior*, Volume 1, 2020.

McGregor, Richard. *Asia's Reckoning: The Struggle for Global Dominance*. Londres: Allen Lane, 2017.

Medcalf, Rory. *Contest for the Indo-Pacific: Why China Won't Map the Future*. Carlton: La Trobe University Press, 2020.

Morceiro, Paulo. *Desindustrialização na economia brasileira no período 2000–2011: abordagens e indicadores*. São Paulo: Editora Cultura Acadêmica, 2012. https://valoradicionado.wordpress.com/2021/06/01/brasil-volta-a-relacao-centro-periferia/.

———. "Brasil volta à relação centro-periferia." January 1, 2021.

Oliveira, Gustavo L.T. de. "The Geopolitics of Brazilian Soybeans." *The Journal of Peasant Studies*, 2015.

Oliveira, Henrique Altemani de. "Brasil e China: uma nova aliança não-escrita?" *Revista Brasileira de Política Internacional*, Volume 53, Issue 2, 2010.

Perez, Ana Cândida. Interview to the author. December 27, 2021.

Prazeres, Tatiana. Interview to the author. July 27, 2021.

Pinheiro-Machado, Rosana. *Counterfeit Itineraries in the Global South: The Human Consequences of Piracy in China and Brazil*. London: Routledge, 2017.

Piza, Douglas de Toledo. "Um pouco da mundialização contada a partir da região da Rua 25 de março: migrantes chineses e comércio 'informal'." Dissertação de mestrado em Sociologia, Universidade de São Paulo, 2012.

Rachman, Gideon. *Easternisation: War and Peace in the Asian Century*. Nova York: Vintage Digital, 2016.

Ray, Rebecca e Gallagher, Kevin. "China in Latin America: Environment and Development Dimensions." *Revista Tempo do Mundo*, Volume 2, Issue 2, Junho de 2016.

Rodrik, Dani. "Premature deindustrialization." *Journal of Economic Growth*, Volume 21, Issue 1, 2016.

Roett, Riordan and Paz, Guadalupe (orgs). *China's Expansion in the Western Hemishphere: Implications for Latin America and the United States*. Brookings Institution Press: Washington, 2008.

Rosito, Tatiana. *Bases para uma Estratégia de Longo Prazo do Brasil para a China*. Rio de Janeiro: Conselho Empresarial Brasil-China, 2020.

Santoro, Maurício. "The Dragon and the Captain: China in the Perspective of Brazil's Nationalist Right." *GEOSUL* (UFSC), Volume 35, 2020.

———. "China in Latin America in the 21st Century." *Cuadernos Iberoamericanos*, Volume 8, 2021.

Scolese, Eduardo and Nossa, Leonencio. *Viagens com o Presidente. Dois repórteres no encalço de Lula do Planalto ao exterior*. Rio de Janeiro: Record, 2006.

Stuenkel, Oliver. *The BRICS and the Future of Global Order*. London: Lexington Books, 2015

———. "Huawei or Not? Brazil Faces a Key Geopolitical Choice." *Americas Quarterly*, June 30, 2020.

Tang, Charles. Interview to the author. September 10, 2021.

Thomaz, Daniel. "Por que a China aposta na língua portuguesa." BBC Brasil, August 23, 2017.

Vigevani, Tullo e Cepaluni, Gabriel. "A Política Externa de Lula da Silva: a estratégia da autonomia pela diversficação." *Contexto Internacional*, Volume 9, Issue 2, 2007.

Wise, Carol. *Dragonomics: How Latin America Is Maximizing (or Missing Out on) China's International Development Strategy.* New Haven: Yale University Press, 2020.

Woods, Randy and Mayeda, Andrew. "Trump Steps Up Efforts to Check China's Influence in Latin America." Bloomberg, January 4, 2018

Yang, Philippe. "O que o Brasil quer da China?" *Valor Econômico,* February 14, 2020.

CHAPTER 3

The Chinese Are Coming: China's Investments in Brazil

This chapter analyzes the role of Chinese Foreign Direct Investment (FDI) in Brazil. It begins with an overview of China's investments in Latin America, showing that they are concentrated in the extraction of natural resources, such as mining and oil, for export to Asia. The section also discusses which countries of the region that receive more FDI from China, noticing that they are few—their concentration is not only in economic sectors, but also in geography. The section ends with a discussion of the Belt and Road Initiative in Latin America, with the mixed results that China so far achieved in the region—20 nations became part of the New Silk Road, but the major countries opted for staying out of the project.

The second section addresses Chinese FDI in Brazil, the major recipient in Latin America, with half of the total. The profile of these investments is slightly different than the ones of the rest of the region, for most of them are in the Brazilian electrical sector, generating, distributing and transmitting energy that is sold to the domestic market. Despite that, Brazil also has China's FDI supporting the export of natural resources, such as in railways connecting mines and agribusiness production to ports.

The third section is a case study of Chinese investments in the Brazilian electrical sector, due to its importance—about half of China's capital stock in the country. The text maps the actions of the main players in the field and discusses why they chose to invest in Brazil, highlighting issues such

© The Author(s), under exclusive license to Springer Nature   47
Singapore Pte Ltd. 2022
M. Santoro, *Brazil–China Relations in the 21st Century*,
https://doi.org/10.1007/978-981-19-0353-3_3

as the positive diplomatic partnership, an open juridical framework and Chinese competitive technological advantages in hydropower.

The following section of the chapter is a brief discussion of Brazil's FDI in China, addressing the reasons why it is so low and mapping the trajectory of the most important Brazilian companies in the country.

Finally, the last part of the chapter addresses the role of culture and soft power in creating bridges between Brazil and China, an attempt to overcome what still is a big distance between the two nations.

3.1   Chinese Investment
in Latin America: An Overview

Chinese investment in Latin America and the Caribbean followed trade. The region became an important trade partner to China in the 2000s, exporting commodities such as soy, iron ore, cooper, oil, meat and wood. By the end of the decade, Chinese firms started to invest in Latin America, usually helping to build and develop the infrastructure to sell these products to Asia. This is part of a larger pattern of China's FDI in the Global South, looking for raw materials and natural resources (Alden 2017; Dent 2010; Eisenman 2015; Evan Ellis 2014; Gallagher 2016; Jenkins 2018; Kaplan 2021; Roett and Paz 2008).

By the end of the 2010s, China's capital stock in the region was US$106 billion, of a total of US$900 billion that the Chinese invested abroad. Chinese investment in Latin American infrastructure was more than the sum of what multilateral financial institutions such as the World Bank and the Inter-American Development Bank had invested in the region (Dollar 2017).

China's FDI in Latin America is very concentrated in a few countries and sectors. Of the 33 nations of the region, over two-thirds of Chinese investment are in Brazil (59%) and Perú (19%), and 96% in them and other five markets: Argentina (10%), Chile (8%), Venezuela (4%), Ecuador (4%) and México (2%). The numbers concern capital stock from 2007 to 2018 (Cariello 2019, p. 22).

Regarding economic sectors, Chinese FDI in Latin America goes mostly to energy (53%) and mining (30%), followed by agriculture (5%) and transportation (5%). However, this data is the result of the huge influence of investments in Brazil's electrical sector. If we exclude the country from the list and take into account only the other Latin American countries, the top positions basically change along similar percentages to mining (51%) and energy (36%). This is a reflection of FDI in Peruvian and Chilean cooper, and Venezuelan and Ecuadorian oil, among other major projects (Cariello 2019, pp. 22–24).

One of the big international discussions about Chinese FDI is if they cause a "debt-trap" problem in developing countries with bad governance, especially the ones which are a part of the Belt and Road Initiative. The concern is that governments will receive loans from China's development banks to finance projects beyond their financial means. Eventually, they will be default and Chinese companies will take control of strategic assets in infrastructure in the Global South.

These discussions are also present in the debates about Latin America, especially concerning Ecuador and Venezuela. As we saw above, Chinese investments are not particularly concentrated in these nations, but the scenario is different regarding official loans. Between 2007 and 2014, China Development Bank and China EximBank in Latin America lent US$118,4 to the region, mostly to Venezuela (53%), followed by Brazil (18%), Argentina (12%) and Ecuador (12%) (Dollar 2017, pp. 6–7).

In the case of Brazil, there is a focus on financing oil extraction. Until 2020, there were 13 Chinese loans to the country, and 12 of them went to Petrobras. Being the largest company of the country, it is a mix-capital firm with the majority of shares owned by the government. China became its major creditor after 2009, due to several causes: the discovery of the huge pre-salt oil fields, the need to find money to exploit them—something more difficult after the global financial crisis—and also Petrobras own financial troubles after it became the center of a corruption scandal in the 2010s (Barbosa 2021).

By the end of the 2010s, China was expanding its Belt and Road Initiative to Latin America. The global project of investment in infrastructure was designed towards Eurasia and Eastern Africa (Drache 2019; Maçães 2018; Mayer 2017; Miller 2017), but as it grew, the Chinese government expanded it to other regions. Its goals in Latin America were roughly the same: to facilitate access to the natural resources and consumer markets important to the development of China (Santoro 2020).

Until 2021, 19 of the 33 countries of Latin America had signed memorandums of understanding and joined the Belt and Road Initiative. Although they are the majority of the countries of the region, they do not represent a strong economic powerbase. Most of them are small nations of Central America and Caribbean, with some South American governments politically close to Beijing, such as Bolivia, Ecuador and

Venezuela. The biggest regional economy in the project is Chile. The major Latin American nations, such as Argentina, Brazil, Colombia and Mexico, which amount to 70% of the GDP of region, are not part of the initiative (Koop 2020).

In other words, there is a gap between the Belt and Road and China's major trade and investment partners in Latin America, which are usually not in the project. Brazil is a good example, with several Brazilian administrations being cautious about the initiative—why take the geopolitical risk, if Chinese FDI is coming in great numbers, anyway?

However, even so the rising presence of China's investment in the region led to reactions from the United States, such as the projects America Growth and Building Back Better, from Donald Trump and Joe Biden's administrations. Americans see the BRI as part of a triangular relation between the United States, China and Latin America (Meyers 2021).

3.2   CHINESE INVESTMENT IN BRAZIL

Brazil is the "jewel in the crown" in China's economic relations with Latin America (Wise 2020, p. 160), and that applies both to trade and to investments. However, there are important differences in Chinese FDI in Brazil in comparison with other countries in the region. The majority of them are in the electric sector, towards the domestic market, and are not dedicated to promote commodities exports to Asia, although this kind of project is also common.

In the comprehensive evaluation of the China-Brazil Business Council, Chinese capital stock in the country was US$66.1 billion in 2020 (Cariello 2021, p. 10), the 25th position among foreign investors in Brazil, although it is rising (Schutte 2020, p. 96). This may sound not much for a 2-trillion dollar GDP, but China's FDI became an important player in many economic sectors, especially in the harsh years after 2014, when Brazil suffered from recession and political instability, with record lows in investment in infrastructure.

The biggest slice of Chinese investment in Brazil is in energy, especially the generation, transmission and distribution of hydropower electrical power, with 48% as we will analyze in Sect. 3.3. In second place, it is the oil and gas sector with 28%, followed by mining (7%), manufacturing (6%), infrastructure (5%) and agriculture (2%) (Cariello 2021, p.10).

China-Brazil Business Council identified 176 projects of Chinese FDI from 2007 to 2020. Almost half of them (48%) were greenfield initiatives, with Chinese companies starting new ventures. This trend became stronger by the end of the decade, because at the time they understood better the complex regulation of the Brazilian market and started to win the auctions for public concessions in infrastructure (Cariello 2019, p. 14, 2021, p. 11).

The other half of the FDI projects were divided between mergers and acquisitions of firms with assets in Brazil (40%) and join-ventures involving Chinese companies with partners in the country (12%) (Cariello 2021, p. 11). In many cases, these brownfield projects were an important part of how China entered the Brazilian market and started the long learning process to navigate its complicated bureaucracy.

Through M&As and joint-ventures, they acquired not only assets in Brazil, but also Brazilian staff, already familiarized with the conditions of the country. This was very important, for in the beginning of the investment—the decade of 2000—Chinese firms usually did not have large experience in internationalization in Latin America, and faced challenges such as the lack of information of Brazilian consumers about China (Cai 2020; Yue 2020).

They also had several advantages. The most important: a positive juridical and political framework for doing business in Brazil, without the tensions and barriers that they often meet in the United States or other developed nations. In the 2000s, the Sino-Brazilian strategic partnership was already an established diplomatic practice and several of Brazil's administrations welcomed China. The Workers' Party, which ruled the country during the global commodity boom, saw Beijing as a trusted partner and an attractive option to reduce dependence from the West.

Since the 1990s, Brazil had implemented several economic reforms that opened the country to foreign trade and investment, eliminating government monopolies, taking away restrictions to FDI and privatizing SOEs (or opening their capital). These measures were important in all the areas where Chinese became key players, such as the electric sector, oil, telecommunications and mining.

Even better: Brazil did not put any restriction on the origin of the FDI. Chinese companies can invest in whatever they want, as long as they comply with the appropriate legislation. There are no forbidden zones due to national security concerns, in contrast to what happens in the United States. There is no equivalent in Brazil to the American Department of

Treasury's Committee on Foreign Investment, which can veto FDI if it understands that there are geopolitical risks. Something it has done in the past, deciding against projects by Arab or Chinese firms, for example.

Is this something that may change? Absolutely. In Chapter 5, we will discuss how China is becoming a partisan issue in Brazilian domestic policy, with the rise of ideological currents hostile to Beijing and advocating the establishment of restrictions to Chinese investment and trade.

The most controversial debate on China's FDI in Brazil has been about Huawei and the 5G Internet pattern. As in other countries, this is a key technology for the next global wave of innovation, and the Sino-American geopolitical conflict regarding its implementation reached Brazil as well, splitting the government among groups that wanted a closer relation with Washington and others who recognized the importance of the issue to Beijing and feared the costs of a veto towards the Chinese company (Stuenkel 2020).

However, Huawei has been investing in Brazil since the 1990s and it is a major supplier of telecommunication equipment both for the State and for the private sector, with many important partnerships with agribusiness and financial sectors and factories in the country. These Brazilian companies defended Huawei. For example, Globo, the most important media group of the country, published newspaper editorials saying that it would be a mistake to exclude the Chinese firm from the 5G (O Globo 2020).

In 2021, Brazil's government authorized Huawei to supply equipment to the companies that took part in the 5G auction, after two years of delays in the decision. The telecommunication firms that will build and operate the new system will thus use Chinese technology. Several factors led to that result, including not only the pressures of the Brazilian private sector but also a higher dependence of Beijing for international health cooperation in the context of the coronavirus pandemic (Costa 2021; see also Chapter 5).

Huawei has been so far an exception in the debates about Chinese FDI in Brazil. The Brazilian scenario is different from the developed nations because of two main reasons. The first is that Brazil does not see China as a geopolitical threat. On the contrary, since the mid-1970s, several Brazilian administrations, from a broad ideological spectrum, perceive Beijing as a strategic partner in a Global South dialogue to build a multipolar world. They see China as part of the solution, not as a problem.

The second motive is dire economic necessity. Since the collapse of the national-developmentalist model in the 1980s, Brazil is hungry for invest-ment in infrastructure. On average, they have been less than 3% per year, in what specialists believe that is below even what is needed to maintain existing assets, not to mention to build new ones (Taylor 2020, p. 45). Without China and other international investors, Brazil faces problems of gaps in the infrastructure for development. In the words of Charles Tang, the president of Brazil-China Chamber of Commerce: "Every Brazilian company wants to marry a rich Chinese" (Tang 2021).

For example, Brazil has just 30,000 km of railways, while China, a country of similar size, has 146,000 km. Just 15% of Brazilian cargo is transported by trains, most of it is iron ore. Since the 1980s, the country has been investing in railways only 0.15 of its GDP per year (Marchetti et al. 2018).

Chinese interest in Brazilian railways has been on the rise since the 2010s, linked with a concern about making it easier and cheaper to export commodities to Asia. The most important railways under construc-tion in Brazil—Ferrogrão, Fico, Fiol—are projects which link mines and agribusiness clusters to the river and seashore ports. This is the type of initiative where China's FDI in the country is closer to the pattern observed in other Latin American nations, of the connections between Chinese investment and the exploitation of natural resources.

However, there are important peculiarities in the Brazilian experience, which highlight the role of a stronger State in establishing the rules for the actions of Chinese companies. They had to adapt to the purposes and goals of Brazil's regulatory framework, changing their initial behavior in a learning curve on how to operate in the country (Abdenur et al. 2021).

The major Chinese players in Brazil's railway market are two SOEs, China Communications Construction Company (CCCC) and China Rail-ways Construction Corporation. They have invested in billionaire projects such as, respectively, the Pará Railway and the East–West Integration Railway (Fiol). Both initiatives fit the pattern of large-scale infrastructure works to connect mines and plantations to the ports.

When China Railways started to operate in Brazil in the 2010s, it proposed to the government the creation of a joint-venture with the Brazilian SOE Valec to build its projects. The federal administration refused. As the minister of Transportation explained to a journalist, the government preferred the established model of an auction, in which many firms would compete to win a public infrastructure concession. The official also said that if he made an exception to Chinese, other players, such as the Russians, would demand the same (Moreira 2016).

The Brazilian framework of auctions for public concessions in infrastructure has been under development since the liberal reforms of the 1990s. In the 2010s, it was organized in the Programa de Parceria de Investimentos (Investments Partnership Program), which organize the auctions for airports, highways, railways and other projects. Chinese companies have to follow its rules, just like the companies from other countries, including the Brazilian ones.

China's SOEs adapted to this scenario hiring Brazilian staff and buying local firms. For example, CCCC bought Brazil's Concremat, a major construction company, to become more competitive in the public auctions. It worked: CCCC won important concessions, such as the management of the Northeast port of São Luís and the contract to build the bridge from the city of Salvador to the island of Itaparica—it will be the biggest bridge in Brazil (Lavoratti 2020).

Chinese SOEs are also interested in Ferrogrão, the most important railway project under discussion in Brazil. It will link the dynamic agribusiness region of the Center West to the Amazon river ports, from where soybean and other products can be exported to Asia. However, it is a complex initiative, with huge social and environmental impacts, going through Indigenous Peoples' lands (Abdenur et al. 2021). To successfully build and manage such railway would be a big challenge for any firm.

3.3   CASE STUDY: CHINESE INVESTMENT IN BRAZIL'S ELECTRICAL SECTOR

Research by Boston University's Center for Global Development discovered that Brazil is the foreign country where China has invested more money in electrical energy. This section analyzes these investments and concludes that what explains Chinese interest in the sector is a combination of Brazilian natural resources and advanced technology that makes China's firms very competitive in this market.

Chinese FDI in Brazil's electrical sector is about US$36.5 billion, the majority of all its investment in the country, around 50%. They are concentrated in hydropower, which is the most important part of the national energy matrix. Almost all of them are the result of SOEs, especially State Grid and China Three Gorges Corporation (Barbosa 2020; Cariello 2019; Schutte 2020).

Both firms have a sizeable part of their foreign assets in Brazil—more than 50% of State Grid and over 30% of China Three Gorges (Schutte 2020, p. 101). It is a fact that deserves explanation, for most of Chinese FDI in electrical energy is usually concentrated in its near abroad, in countries that are part of the Belt and Road Initiative and have close ties to Beijing, such as Pakistan. The high level of commitment to the South American nation shows the strength of the Sino-Brazilian partnership and how it helped to pave way to the investments.

Chinese FDI in Brazil started to grow after the 2008 global financial crisis and the intensification of China's Going Global policy to stimulate the internationalization of its firms. In the 2010s, Brazil became the 5th top recipient of its FDI, behind United States, Australia, United Kingdom and Switzerland. In general terms, this was a good macroeconomic time for Brazilians, with good levels of growth and low inflation. Political stability and the creation of BRICS also helped to make Brazil more attractive to Chinese capital and to ensure Beijing of a positive diplomatic environment.

Another important factor was the changes in Brazil's juridical framework, which created an open scenario for FDI, no matter its national origin. In the 1990s and 2000s, Brazilian presidents implemented liberal reforms which opened the electrical sector to foreign companies. The Chinese were part of a larger trend (Vanderlei 2018).

China was well positioned to take advantage of the new conditions, for the hydropower sector was an important part of Sino-Brazilian relations since the 1980s. At the time, one of the goals of Deng Xiaoping's Four Modernizations policy was the expansion and transformation of the electrical sector. The Chinese perceived Brazil as an important reference due to its excellence in engineering and to the success of high-profile public works such as the Itaipu dam—then, the biggest of the world (Cai 2020).

In one generation, the Chinese reversed the trend and became themselves the teachers to Brazilians. They developed a sophisticated technology called ultra-high voltage transmission (UHF), which allows for cheaper, safer and cleaner conduction of electricity through large distances (Cohen 2019). State Grid and China Three Gorges became firms with a high degree of internationalization, operating in many countries and environments, well financed by Chinese development banks.

China's companies entered the Brazilian electrical market in the 2010s. SOEs were responsible for 98% of these investments. Although there are 14 Chinese firms in this sector in Brazil, State Grid and China Three Gorges concentrate 83% of the total amount (Barbosa 2020).

The two giants started their presence in the country through brownfield investments, buying shares or assets from European companies from Spain and Portugal which already had Brazilian concessions. By doing that, they acquired local staff with expertise about Brazil's complex legislation and local conditions (Cai 2020). This was especially important because the biggest infrastructure projects in the country are usually public concessions, which are won through competitive auctions.

Chinese companies learned how to do it (see the section above, for the example of railways), and in the case of State Grid, the watershed was winning in 2015 the auction to build the transmission line from the Belo Monte dam, in the Amazon, to the big consumer markets in the Southeast. It is a case that illustrates well the comparative advantaged of the firm in Brazil (Cai 2020; Cohen 2019).

The transmission line has over 2,500 km and goes through three different ecosystems: the Amazon, the savannah of the Cerrado and the Atlantic rainforest. It was a complex engineering project with huge social and environmental impacts, demanding negotiations with social movements, Indigenous Peoples, individual landowners and several layers of government in different Brazilian states.

State Grid was able to complete the project successfully because of its local expertise, but also because it had lots of experience with similar transmission lines in China, where conditions look a lot like Brazil, in the sense that the power dams are usually far away from the consumers.

Another major operation of State Grid in Brazil was buying the majority of the shares in Companhia Paulista de Força e Luz (CPFL) in 2017. The company is the major distributor of electric energy in the country, especially in the Southeast and in the South, the richest regions. It was a good example of a transaction that would probably be forbidden in the United States, due to concerns about national security. However, in Brazil, it did not raise political concerns, and State Grid usually receives good press as an competent company.

The other major Chinese investor in the sector, China Three Gorges, has a similar history in Brazil. It entered the national market in 2012 through the acquisition of the majority of shares of the Portuguese firm EDP Energias, which had asset in the countries. In the following years, it went into a buying spree of several power dams that left China Three Gorges, the second biggest generator of electric energy in Brazil, only behind the Brazilian SOE Eletrobras.[1]

Chinese FDI in Brazil electric sector is 80% concentrated in hydropower, although China Three Gorges also invests in solar and wind energy, benefiting from Brazilian government financial incentives (Barbosa 2020). In that sense, Brazil is also a testing ground for new technologies and practices that could be applied in the future in China itself. As Beijing deepens it commitment to the green economy and pledges to be carbon–neutral in 2060, its Brazilian investments in sustainable development may become even more important (Studart and Myers 2020).

Chinese FDI in Brazil electrical sector presents important differences from its typical investments in developing countries discussed at the beginning of this chapter. They are not about build infrastructure for commodities exports to Asia. Their focus is to generate and/or transmit energy to the Brazilian domestic market. Although they exploit a natural resource (water), they are capital-intensive operations with advanced technology, including applications that could be, later, used in China. It as a process of "modernization through globalization" (Kong 2019), in which internationalization stimulates firms to innovate.

Another main difference is that Chinese companies in Brazil's electrical sector use mostly local staff, instead of taking to the country huge numbers of employees from China—those are usually limited to the management group. The local expertise has been fundamental to operate in Brazilian complex legal system, with many labor and environmental obligations, and in the competitive auctions for infrastructure concessions, part of a 10-year learning curve of Chinese firms in South America (Abdenur et al. 2021).

3.4   BRAZILIAN INVESTMENTS IN CHINA

Brazil's FDI in China is of a much smaller size than the opposite. In 2019, before the outbreak of the coronavirus pandemic, there were 78 Brazilian companies present in the Asian country, in comparison with over 200 Chinese firms in Brazil (Lavoratti 2020). Between 2000 and 2010, they

---

[1] Complete list available at company's website: https://www.ctgbr.com.br/negocios/. Access in February 2021.

had invested US$572 million in China, 0.04% of the foreign capital stock in the country (Frischtak and Soares 2012). There is nothing in the scale, for example, of State Grid's FDI in Latin America.

In the 1990s, Brazilian construction companies had huge ambitions in China, with the expectation that they would apply their expertise in Itaipu and other big projects to build the Three Gorges Dam. They opened offices in Beijing and invested heavily on public relations. However, they failed to win major contracts. The Chinese government reserved Three Gorges and other infrastructure works to its own SOEs, and the Brazilian firms got only minor consulting tasks (Biato Junior 2010; Spitzcovsky 2021).

The presence of the Brazilian firms in China is usually restricted to offices of representation (40%) for sales and other services (36.8%). Just 14% are factories (Frischtak and Soares 2012). In geographical terms, they are concentrated in the big cities (Beijing, Shanghai) and seashore provinces (Jiangsu, Shandong, Zhejiang), with little presence in the interior.

The presence in the local market is very important for Brazilian companies in order to access the Chinese consumers. There are many specific cultural characteristics of China's market that can only be grasped by firms operating there (Prazeres 2021).

Most of them invest in the services sector (50.9%), with a significant participation in industrial manufacture (28.1%) and transformation of natural resources, such as agribusiness and oil (21%) (Frischtak and Soares 2012). It is a very different pattern of Chinese FDI in Brazil, which is concentrated in energy.

Petrobras has been the pioneer among Brazilian firms in China, exploiting oil wells in the 1980s, in partnership with BP (Pimentel 2009, pp. 96–106). At the time, the Chinese were major exporters of the commodities, the most important item that it sold to Brazil.

However, the relationship of the company with China changed with time, as the pattern of the bilateral trade was reversed and the Chinese became major oil importers. In 2004, when president Lula visited the country, Petrobras opened an office of representation. It started negotiations with China's oil SOEs, the only firms authorized to buy oil (Frischtak and Soares 2012).

Instead of Petrobras investing in Chinese extraction of hydrocarbons, the opposite happened, with China's financial institutions lending money to it, in order to exploit the pre-salt fields, as discussed in Sect. 3.1 (Barbosa 2021).

In contrast, Embraco has a more stable story of manufacturing in China. The Brazilian firm's specialization is the making of compressors, used in refrigeration. Embraco began its operations in China in the 1980s, selling to the People's Republic through tradings in Hong Kong. In 1995, it negotiated a joint-venture with a Beijing municipal SOE and started a factory. With time, it became a major operation that even led to changes in the products of the company, with the development of more silent compressors, due to the Chinese costume of putting the fridges in the living room (Pimentel 2009, pp. 65–75).

Brazilian multinationals invested in China for two main reasons: access to the Chinese consumer market and/or to remain competitive globally, with better supply chains, cheaper labor costs and economies of scale (Fleury 2021).

This process of internationalization in China was never easy, and Brazilian companies suffered from many problems: lack of knowledge about the country, inadequate training for its staff, cultural conflicts between Brazil's executives and Chinese employees. They also complain about insufficient support from the Brazilian government in dealing with the complexity of China's laws and bureaucratic regulation, especially difficulties regarding intellectual property (Frischtak and Soares 2012; Silva 2020).

Another point, highlighted by former secretary of Foreign Trade, Welber Barral, is the lack of a "Brazil brand" among Chinese consumers. They usually do not have a very developed idea of the country and its products, which make it harder for its firms to consolidate its presence in Asia (Barral 2021).

Embraer's somewhat turbulent trajectory in China is a good example. The Brazilian airplane company operates globally and it is very competitive in the market of executive jets. It negotiated a joint-venture with Chinese SOE Avic II and built a factory in Harbin, aiming to produce to China's regional market. It was a lucrative operation that helped to sustain for years some of Embraer's models (Castro Neves 2021).

But it was always a complicated deal, with another SOE, Avic I, launching similar jets and hiring former Embraer employees (Pimentel 2009, pp. 75–86; Lavoratti 2020). When Boeing negotiated buying Embraer, the operations in China were suspended, but were resumed after the deal with the American company failed (Fleury 2021).

3.5   The Role of Culture
in Sino-Brazilian Relations

Brazil and China are distant countries, in terms of both geography and culture. In this book, many businesspeople, politicians and officials described how this lack of a better understanding makes it harder for the two societies to establish closer relations and to find and exploit trade and investment opportunities. This section addresses the role of culture in overcoming the "tyranny of distance" which disturbs Brazil's ties with Asian nations (Pfeiffer 2017). That is: how being far away, in terms of both geography and cultural traditions, makes these relationships more difficult.

Before the reform and opening period, the cultural exchanges between Brazil and the People's Republic of China were limited, usually restricted to personal contacts among Brazilian communist intellectuals and their Chinese counterparts—after all, Brasília just recognized the PRC in 1974, so most dialogues happened only among the international networks of the Communist Party.

For example, Beijing's authorities translated and published writer Jorge Amado and the celebrated poet Ai Qing visited Brazil in 1954, as part of his Latin American tour. He liked the country and wrote poems about it, but also faced obstacles in his trip due to anticommunism (Ai 2019). In the 1960s, Brazilian journalist Jaime Martins moved to Beijing to work for China's state media and for several decades was the only professional of the country working there in that capacity, raising his family among the turmoil of the Cultural Revolution (Machado 2020).

During the Cold War, Brazil was the home of Zhang Daqian, the greatest Chinese painter of the last one hundred years. He went to Latin America as a refugee of the Revolution of 1949 and lived in a small ranch in the state of São Paulo, where he planted a traditional garden and built his studio. However, after his death, his farm was flooded by the construction of a dam. A new generation of artists is giving more attention to his memory and life story, and trying to identify his works in Brazilian museums (Patrick 2021).

With the beginning of the reform and opening process in 1978, contemporary Chinese culture became to be more present in Brazil, with the arrival of the films of the new generation of directors, such as Zhang Yimou and Chen Kaige, and Brazilian editions of important modern writers such as Lu Xun, Mo Yan and Yu Hua. Brazilian diplomat Ricardo

Portugal selected and translated an anthology of classical poetry from the Tang dynasty (Portugal and Tan 2013).

Nonetheless, in the twenty-first century, China's cultural presence in Brazil is low, much below what could be expected in comparison with the huge economic influence and the political meaning of the strategic partnership. Chinese literature, movies or music are not popular and well known in the country (Stuenkel 2018). It is part of a "soft power deficit" in Sino-Latin American relations (Meyers and Wise 2016), and it has been the subject of recent efforts in "people-to-people diplomacy" from the PRC (Meyers 2021).

There are some important initiatives in the field which highlight how important culture can be to improve the bilateral relationship. Paulo Menechelli Filho, who researches the issue, highlights that culture can be a tool to reduce fears, xenophobia and mistrust (Menechelli Filho 2021).

China's most important tool of cultural diplomacy in the Confucius Institute was created in 2004. It develops partnerships with local universities around the world—currently, there are more than 500, in 146 countries. Their creation was part of a broader movement by the Hu Jintao administration (2002–2012) in encouraging the internationalization of Chinese companies, the expansion abroad of its State media (Xinhua, CGTN) and the diffusion of the country's culture (Barr 2011; Becard and Menechelli Filho 2019; Gil 2017; Hubbert 2019, Kingsley et al. 2019. Kurlanyzick 2007).

In Brazil, there are Confucius Institutes in a dozen cities, mostly in state capitals or university towns. Qiao Jianzhen was the director of Rio de Janeiro's Confucius Institute, a partnership with the Catholic University (PUC-Rio), a private institution. She started to study Portuguese in the 1990s and worked as an interpreter before coming to Brazil in 2012 to take charge of the organization. In the eight years, she lived in the country she traveled to several cities, implementing educational and cultural projects (Qiao 2020, 2021).

Qiao belongs to the fourth generation of her family who works as a teacher, and she believes that education is a long-term process: "You need 10 years to cultivate a tree, and 100 years to develop a person" (Qiao 2021). In Brazil, she established courses on Chinese culture and language, and engaged students in international competitions—one of them. Monica Cunha da Silva, won the Chinese Bridge Proficiency contest in 2014, the first Latin American to do so (Qiao 2020).

Qiao highlights that China can be a very distant country for her students, especially the ones who are from poor families. Because of that, she says that projects which address this social group touched her the most during her stay in Brazil. Two initiatives of this type were the establishment of Mandarin classes at public school in a poor neighborhood in the metropolitan zone of Rio, Colégio Matemático Joaquim Gomes de Souza. One hundred of its students and teachers went to China with scholarships or exchange programs. Other project was a summer camp in the Asian country for young football players, many of which went back to train at Chinese universities (Qiao 2021), part of the national efforts under Xi Jinping of being a global sport power.

Although in the United States and in Europe Confucius Institutes have been the target of many suspicious of espionage and political conflicts regarding the spreading of ideological tensions between China and the West (Becard and Menechelli Filho 2019; Gil 2017; Hubbert 2019), nothing of the sort has happened in Brazil. They are usually seen in a positive light, as the cultural diplomacy of the biggest trade partner of the country. Also, Confucius Institutes in Brazil are increasingly using Brazilian teachers—sometimes, such as in Brasília, all the staff (Menechelli Filho 2021).

Mandarin teachers are also playing an important role in people-to-people diplomacy, sometimes becoming digital influencers with hundreds of thousands of followers of their posts on Chinese culture. This is the case of Wang Yili and Si Lao. Both are Chinese immigrants in Brazil, and their profiles on TikTok, YouTube and other social media apps are important references for Brazilians interested in China. Both have been the subject of portraits in the media (Carbinato 2021; Zhang 2021).

Wang Yili and her mother, Liou Sheaujian, were also actresses in the movie "Made in China." Starred by the famous Brazilian comedian Regina Casé, it tells the story of a group of Brazilian and Chinese small shopkeepers of Rio's popular shopping district Rua da Alfândega learning to work together, accepting each other culture and developing a business partnership.

It is possible to study Mandarin in Brazil outside the Confucius Institutes—for example, at private course. But there is just one undergraduate course in Chinese at Brazilian universities, at University of São Paulo. It offers a four-year degree along in three lines: language, literature and culture. The movie director Milena de Moura is one of the students who completed the course and then moved to China to do a master at the Beijing Film Academy. Her trajectory is a good example of the possibilities of this cultural dialogue.

Milena's interest in Chinese culture began because of acupuncture, which opened the door for a more general curiosity about China's traditions. At university, she studied poetry and literature and went for an exchange program in the city of Xian. Her stay in Asia transformed her artistic views, through the contact with artists who were more diverse in their methods than their Western colleagues, usually working in several mediums, such as painting, cinema and poetry (Moura 2021).

Moving to China and to film school for her graduate studies, Milena got a degree at documentary, and her first movie as a director was "Canções em Pequim" [Songs in Beijing]. She applied the techniques and ideas of Brazilian filmmaker Eduardo Coutinho, asking Chinese people to sing songs which were important for them, that somehow touched their lives. It was also a way to look for common ground on Brazilian and Chinese culture, due to their love of music. Then, she turned to soybeans, producing the podcast "Grão" [Grain] and starting a documentary of its role in the bilateral relationship (Moura 2021).

Chinese State Media is present in Brazil, with local offices of Xinhua New Agency and correspondents for the People's Daily, Radio China International and CGTN TV. They have agreements with Brazilian media to share their content, although Brazil's press usually prefers to do so with their Western colleagues.

There a few exceptions, such as TV Bandeirantes, which since 2019 airs stories in partnership with the China Media Group. Specialists usually consider their influence and audience in Brazil to be small. They point that official exchange programs which take to Asia Brazilian politicians and scholars are much more influential in shaping the country's elite perception of China.[2]

If the expansion of the Chinese media in Brazil is a part of a larger State project of a rising power, the Brazilian journalist coverage of China is more erratic, and it often reflects the personal choices of a few individuals interested in the Asian country. In the 1990s, Jaime Spitzcovsky suggested to the publisher of newspaper Folha de São Paulo to be sent to China, after his stint in Russia, arguing that it was important to report on the rise of the new great power of the twenty-first century (Spitzcovsky 2021). At

[2] Workshop "The Belt and Road in Latin America: views from the region." CEBRI/Council on Foreign Relations, November 4 and 5, 2020.

the time, he was the only journalist in Beijing writing for Brazil's press, although Brazilian journalist Jaime Martins was working for the Chinese State media.

The global commodity boom of the 2000s, the creation of the BRICS and a relatively more open political climate in China in the mood of hosting the Summer Olympics of 2008 created something of a "golden age" for Brazilian correspondents in the country, with the major national media sending journalists to work in the country. Some of them, such as Claudia Trevisan and Sônia Bridi, wrote books about the experience (Bridi 2008; Trevisan 2009) and continued to be part of the Sino-Brazilian dialogue—Claudia Trevisan, for example, became the secretary executive of the Brazil-China Business Council.

Due to the economic crisis in Brazil in the 2010s, local media outlets reduced their staff abroad, usually maintaining permanent correspondents just in Brazilian traditional diplomatic partners, such as the United States or Argentina. For other nations, they preferred to use the services of international new agencies or freelance reporters. The few journalists from Brazil working in China were generally reporting part-time, while doing graduate school at Chinese universities, or were living in the country accompanying a husband or wife.

In the same pattern, Chinese cultural diplomacy is becoming more important in Brazil, part of a long-term effort of Beijing. The opposite is not true. Brazilian cultural breakouts in China happened a few times, but despite the official policy of Brasília. It was often the result of individual actions.

Arguably, the most famous Brazilian artist in China is actress Lucélia Santos, the star of world-popular TV soap opera "Isaura the Slave Girl," with its powerful story of injustice and hope in nineteenth-century Imperial Brazil. It was shown on Chinese television in the 1980s and Lucélia visited Beijing and other major cities, received prizes and developed a life-long friendship with Chinese audiences (Liu 2020).

"Isaura" was a production of Brazil's Globo Media Group. Although it sells its shows to several countries, its internationalization production process has not been strong, usually limited to a few projects with Portugal. Globo never exploited the possibility of investing in the Chinese market, due to the need of establishing joint-ventures with local TV stations.

There are other examples of one-time hits of Brazilian artists in China which Brazil's government or companies did not exploit. One case is the country singers Milionário and José Rico, who were popular in the 1980s. "Estrada da Vida" (The Road of Life), a documentary about their life and careers, was a surprising success among the Chinese audience, perhaps because they identified themselves with the rural origins and the rags-to-riches story of the Latin American duo. However, Brazilian elites usually despise country music, and the ministries of Foreign Affairs and Culture did not use the opportunity to boost their cultural diplomacy in China.[3]

Another example is the 1968 novel "Meu Pé de Laranja Lima" (My Sweet Orange Tree), by José Mauro de Vasconcelos, a beloved classic of Brazilian children literature. It was translated to Chinese in 2010 and quickly became a best seller in the country.[4] The novel received several awards and it is often quoted by teachers as one of their top choices for classes. It was also mentioned in a popular South Korean soap opera, which helped to increase its popularity (Li 2020).

What explains such success? Perhaps because China's readers felt much in common with the story that the author tells about childhood poverty and the love for nature. A nostalgic longing for the earth that appeals to societies which made a fast transition from rural to urban, such as Brazil and China in the twentieth century. That may be an important roadmap to improve Sino-Brazilian cultural ties.

REFERENCES

Abdenur, Adriana. e Gonzalez Levaggi, Ariel. "Trans-Regional Cooperation in a Multipolar World: how is the Belt and Road Initiative Relevant to Latin America?" *London School of Economics Global South Unit: Working Paper Series*, Issue 1, 2018.
Abdenur, Adriana, Folly, Maiara, and Santoro Maurício. *What Railway Deals Taught Chinese and Brazilians in the Amazon*. Washington: Carnegie Endowment for International Peace, 2021.
Ai Qing. *Viagem à América do Sul*. São Paulo: Editora Unesp, 2019.
Alden, Chris, et al. (orgs). *China and Africa: Building Peace and Security Cooperation on the Continent*. Londres: Palgrave Macmillan, 2017.
Barbosa, Pedro Henrique. Brazil-China Oil Cooperation: Bilateral Trade, FDI, Construction Projects and Loans (2000–2018).

---

[3] Researcher Marcos Queiroz published the story of Milionário, José Rico and China on his Twitter profile: https://twitter.com/marcosvlqueiroz/status/1395783448061677571. Access in November 2021.

[4] I thank Igor Patrick de Souza for calling my attention to this issue.

————. "New Kids on the Block: China's arrival in Brazil's Electric Sector." *Global China Initiative Working Paper 12*, December 2020.

————. "Chinese Economic Statecraft and China's Oil Development Finance in Brazil." *Journal of Current Chinese Affairs*, Volume 50, Issue 3, 2021.

Barr, Michael. *Who's Afraid of China? The Challenge of Chinese Soft Power*. London: Zed Books, 2011.

Barral, Welber. Interview to the author. July 23, 2021.

Becard, Danielly and Menechelli Filho, Paulo. "Chinese Cultural Diplomacy: Instruments in China's Strategy for International Insertion in the 21st Century". *Revista Brasileira de Política Internacional*, Volume 62, Issue 1, 2019.

Biato Júnior, Oswaldo. *A Parceria Estratégica Sino-Brasileira: origens, evolução e perspectivas (1993–2006)*. Brasília: Funag, 2010.

Brautigam, Deborah. e Rithmire, Meg. "The Chinese Debt Trap Is a Myth". *The Atlantic*, February 6, 2021.

Bridi, Sônia. *Laowai: histórias de uma repórter brasileira na China*. Florianópolis: Letras Brasileiras, 2008.

Brito, Cleiton Ferreira Maciel. "Made in China / Produzido no Polo Industrial da Zona Franca de Manaus: o trabalho nas fábricas chinesas." PhD dissertation, Graduate School of Sociology, Federal University of São Carlos, 2017.

Cai, Hongxian. "Nove anos de trabalhos duros no Brasil: a história de crescimento da State Grid Corporation no Brasil." In: Zhou Zhiwei e Wu Changsheng (eds) *Histórias de Amizade entre China e Brasil*. Beijing: China International Press, 2020.

Cariello, Tulio. *Investimentos Chineses no Brasil: histórico, tendências e desafios globais (2007-2020)*. Rio de Janeiro: CEBC, 2021.

————. *Investimentos Chineses no Brasil 2018: o quadro brasileiro em perspectiva global*. Rio de Janeiro: Conselho Empresarial Brasil-China, 2019.

Carbinatto, Bruno. "Conheça a Pula Muralha, startup de ensino de mandarim que nasceu de um canal do YouTube." *Você S/A*, August 19, 2021.

Castro Neves, Luiz Augusto. Interview to the author. December 28, 2021.

Chaisse, J. (org). *China's International Investment Strategy: Bilateral, Regional, and Global Law and Policy*. Oxford: Oxford University Press, 2019.

China. *China's Policy Paper on Latin America and the Caribbean*. Beijing: Ministry of Foreign Affairs, 2016.

Colectivo sobre Financiamiento e Inversiones Chinas, Derechos Humanos y Ambiente (CICDHA). *Tercer Ciclo de la Evaluación Periódica Universal de la República Popular de China desde Sociedad Civil*. CICDHA, 2021.

Cohen, Sandra. "Como a State Grid se tornou a líder do setor elétrico brasileiro." *Época Negócios*, July 12, 2019.

Correa, Germano. e Barbosa Pedro Henrique. "Uma Tentativa Brasileira de Entender o Funcionamento do Governo e do Setor Privado na China." In: P. H. Barbosa (org) *Os Desafios e Oportunidades na Relação Brasil-Ásia na Perspectiva de Jovens Diplomatas*. Brasília: Funag, 2017.

Costa, Ana Clara. "Lição das Bravatas: os bastidores de como o governo cedeu à chinesa Huawei." *Piauí*, Edição 182, 2021.

Dent, Cristopher. *China-Africa Development Relations*. London: Routledge, 2010.

Dollar, David. *China's Investment in Latin America*. Washington: Brookings Institution, 2017.

Drache, D. *One Road, Many Dreams: China's Bold Plan to Remake the Global Economy*. London: Bloomsbury, 2019.

Dussel Peters, Enrique (ed). *China's Financing in Latin America and the Caribbean*. Mexico City: Unam, 2019.

Eisenman, Joshua. *China and the Developing World: Beijing's Strategy for the Twenty-First Century*. London: Routledge, 2015.

Evan Ellis, Robert. *China on the Ground in Latin America: Challenges for the Chinese and Impacts on the Region*. Nova York: Palgrave Macmillan, 2014.

Fleury, Maria Tereza. "A Presença das Multinacionais Brasileiras em Território Chinês." *GVExecutivo*, Volume 20, Issue 2, April 2021.

Frischtak, Claudio and Soares, André. *Empresas Brasileiras na China: presença e experiência*. Rio de Janeiro: Conselho Empresarial Brasil-China, 2012.

Gallagher, Kevin. *The China Triangle: Latin America's China Boom and the Fate of the Washington Consensus*. Nova York: Oxford University Press, 2016.

Gil, Jeffrey. *Soft Power and Worldwide Promotion of Chinese Language Learning: The Confucius Institute Project*. Multilingual Matters Limited, 2017.

Hubbert, Jennifer. *China in the World: An Anthropology of Confucius Institutes, Soft Power and Globalization*. University of Hawaii Press, 2019.

Jenkins, R. *How China Is Reshaping the Global Economy: Development Impacts in Africa and Latin America*. Oxford: Oxford University Press, 2018.

Kaplan, Stephen. *Globalizing Patient Capital: The Political Economy of Chinese Investment in the Americas*. Cambridge: Cambridge University Press, 2021.

Kingsley, Edney, Rosen, Stanley and Zhu Ying (eds). *Soft Power with Chinese Characteristics: China's Campaign for Hearts and Minds*. London: Routledge, 2019.

Kong, Bo. *Modernization Through Globalization: Why China Finances Foreign Energy Projects Worldwide*. Londres: Palgrave, 2019.

Koop. Fermin. "Coronavirus Reshapes Belt and Road in Latin America." *Diálogo Chino*, July 30, 2020.

Kurlanyzick, Joshua. *Charm Offensive: How China's Soft Power Is Transforming the World*. New Haven: Yale University Press, 2007.

Lavoratti, Liliana. "O Trem Para o Futuro." *China Hoje*, December 30th, 2020.

Lee, Ching Kwan. *The Specter of Global China: Politics, Labor, and Foreign Investment in Africa*. Chicago: University of Chicago Press, 2018.

Li Li. "O Meu Pé de Laranja Lima na China: recepção e tradução." *Diacrítica*, Volume 34, Issue 3, 2020.

Liu Jingyan. "Adorável Isaura." In: Zhou Zhiwei e Wu Changsheng (eds) *Histórias de Amizade entre China e Brasil*. Beijing: China International Press, 2020.

Maçães, Bruno. *Belt and Road: The Sinews of Chinese Power*. Boston: C Hurst & Co Publishers Ltd, 2018.

Machado, Marcelo. *A Ponte de Bambu*. Documentary. Brazil, 2020.

Marchetti, Dalmo et al. "Logística." In: Fernando Puga and Lavinia Barros de Castro (eds) *Visão 2035: Brasil, país desenvolvido*. Rio de Janeiro: Banco Nacional de Desenvolvimento Econômico e Social, 2018.

Mayer, Maximilian. *Rethinking the Silk Road: China's Belt and Road Initiative and Emerging Eurasian Relations*. London: Palgrave Macmillan, 2017.

Menechelli Filho, Paulo. Interview to the author. September 17, 2021.

Meyers, Magaret. Interview to the author. September 13, 2021.

Meyers, Margaret and Wise, Carol (eds). *The Political Economy of China-Latin America Relations in the New Millennium*. London: Routledge, 2016.

Miller, Tom. *China's Asian Dream: Empire Building Along the New Silk Road*. London, 2017.

Moreira, Assis. "China Propõe Ao Brasil Criar Estatal Binacional Para Construir Ferrovia." *Valor Econômico*, September 2nd, 2016.

Moura, Milena de. Interview to the author. September 27, 2021.

O Globo. "É um erro excluir a chinesa Huawei do leilão da telefonia celular 5G." *O Globo*, October 21st, 2020.

Patrick, Igor. "Com passagem pelo Brasil, 'Picasso chinês' vai ganhar documen-tário." *Folha de São Paulo*, May 6, 2021.

Pfeifer, Henry. "Brasil e Austrália: além da tirania da distância." In: P. H. Barbosa (ed) *Os Desafios e Oportunidades na Relação Brasil-Ásia na Perspectiva de Jovens Diplomatas*. Brasília: Funag, 2017.

Pimentel, José Eduardo Albino. *Empresas brasileiras na China: estratégia e gestão*. MA dissertation, Faculty of Economy, Administration and Accountancy, University of São Paulo, 2009.

Portugal, Ricardo and Tan, Xiao. *Antologia da Poesia Clássica Chinesa – dinastia Tang*. São Paulo: Editora Unesp, 2013.

Prazeres, Tatiana. Interview to the author. July 27, 2021.

Qiao Jianzhen. Interview to the author. September 23, 2021.

———. "Eu e o Instituto Confúcio no Rio." In: Zhou Zhiwei e Wu Changsheng (eds) *Histórias de Amizade entre China e Brasil*. Beijing: China International Press, 2020.

Roett, Riordan and Paz, Guadalupe (eds). *China's Expansion in the Western Hemisphere: implications for Latin America and the United States.* Washington: Brookings Institution Press, 2008.

Santoro, Maurício. "China in Latin America in the 21st Century." *Cuadernos Iberoamericanos.*

———. "The Dragon and the Captain: China in the Perspective of Brazil's Nationalist Right." *Geosul*, Volume 35, Issue 77, 2020.

Schutte, Giorgio. Romano. *Oásis para o capital - solo fértil para a 'corrida do ouro': a dinâmica dos investimentos produtivos chineses no Brasil.* Curitiba: Appris Editora, 2020.

Silva, Lucia Anderson Ferreira da. *Executivos brasileiros na China: adaptação e dificuldades em empresas brasileiras.* PhD dissertation, Institute of Philosophy and Human Sciences, State University of Campinas, 2020.

Spitzcovsky, Jaime. Interview to the author, July 12, 2021.

Studart, Rogerio. e Myers, Margareth. "Reimagining China-Brazil Relations Under the BRI: The Climate Imperative." *CFR/CEBRI Working Paper*, Washington/Rio de Janeiro, 2020.

Stuenkel, Oliver. "Most Latin Americans Can't Name a Chinese Singer. Why That's Great for Beijing." *Americas Quarterly*, May 1, 2018.

———. "Huawei or Not? Brazil Faces a Key Geopolitical Choice." *Americas Quarterly*, June 30th, 2020.

Tang, Charles. Interview to the author. September 10, 2021.

Trevisan, Claudia. *Os Chineses*. São Paulo: Contexto, 2009.

Taylor, Matthew. *Decadent Developmentalism: The Political Economy of Democratic Brazil.* Cambridge: Cambridge University Press, 2020.

Vanderlei, G. *State Grid: a inserção chinesa no setor elétrico brasileiro.* MA Dissertation, Programme of Graduate Studies in Public Management and International Cooperation. Federal University of Paraíba, 2018.

Wise, Carol. *Dragonomics: How Latin America Is Maximizing (or Missing Out on) China's International Development Strategy.* New Haven: Yale University Press, 2020.

Zhang Rong. "Wang Yili: "influencer" chinesa popular no TikTok divulga história e cultura da China para o mundo." *People's Daily*, Portuguese edition, August 15, 2021.

Yue, Haiping. "Depois De 18 Anos, o Brasil é Como a Minha 'Casa'." In: Zhiwei Zhou and Changsheng Wu (eds) *istórias De Amizade Entre China e Brasil.* Beijing: China Intercontinental Press, 2020.

CHAPTER 4

China, the Amazon and Climate Diplomacy

In the twenty-first century, with the strengthening of its economic relations with Brazil, China became for the first time a major player in the Amazon, as a consumer of the natural resources of the rainforest, as an important investor in its infrastructure and as a Brazilian partner in global climate change negotiations. Beijing is also consolidating itself as one of the great powers which will draft international regulations on what conditions Amazon's products, such as soybeans and meat, will reach foreign markets.

The first section of this chapter tells the economic history of the Amazon, explaining how the region has been since the beginning of European colonization in the sixteenth century, a provider of agricultural or mining goods to international markets, often subject to the effects of short-term global booms, such as rubber.

The emphasis of the section is the regional model of development implemented by the Brazilian military dictatorship in 1970s, which opened the way to agribusiness, cattle and mining, which would become the cornerstones of the Sino-Brazilian trade. The text argues that this new dynamic is marked by a double movement, of rising economic interests in tension with growing concerns about the environment.

The second section addresses the impacts of China in the Amazon, both the positive and the negative effects, discussing how Chinese demand for soybeans and meat stimulates the deforestation, the role of

M. Santoro, *Brazil–China Relations in the 21st Century*,
https://doi.org/10.1007/978-981-19-0353-3_4

its infrastructure investments for the regional economy and the socioenvironmental conflicts in the region. It also discusses how China can play a constructive leadership in setting international standards and rules to curb illegal practices in the Amazon.

The last section deals with the Sino-Brazilian dialogue in climate diplomacy, analyzing how both nations assumed since the 2010s a more active role in the fight about global warming, and the implications of that for how their relationship in the Amazon, such as joint actions against deforestation.

4.1   The Economic Expansion in the Amazon

The Amazon occupies half of the territory of Brazil, but it is the home of the just 10% of the country's population. Historically, it has been an economic space devoted to the exploitation of natural resources in high demand in foreign markets and a geopolitical concern to Portuguese and Brazilian governments, which were afraid that great powers from outside Latin America would take possession of the region (Souza 2019).

In colonial times, the Portugal's empire settled the Amazon along its great river valleys, relying on the Catholic Church orders to do missionary work and to rally Indigenous Peoples to villages and towns. In strategic points of the basin, the Portuguese built military forts, which became the starting point for major cities such as Belém and Manaus.

From an economic point of view, the Portuguese were interested in exploiting a group of spices and agricultural products known by the generic name of "Drogas do sertão" (hinterland's drugs), such as cocoa, guarana, indigo, nuts, pepper, urucum and vanilla. These drugs were usually extracted by Indigenous Peoples' labor, under the Catholic missions or by the Portuguese colonists. Cocoa was by far the most important, representing more than half of the region's exports in the eighteenth and early nineteenth centuries (Harris 2015).

Several Europeans powers were interested in the Amazon and fought the Portuguese for control over it or built their own colonies in the region: France, Great Britain, the Netherlands. This led to a strong feeling in Portugal and later in independent Brazil, that the region was a dangerous geopolitical mix of rich natural resources and demographic void, and that the State should integrate it with the rest of national society. Actually, from the administrative and political perspective the Amazon was a different colony—the state of Grão-Pará and Maranhão—from the rest of Brazil, for reasons of military security.

The new independent Brazilian state incorporated the Amazon, but it was a turbulent region, impoverished and marked by racial conflicts. In the 1830s, it was the stage of the Cabanagem rebellion, a fight between Indigenous Peoples, Black slaves and White Brazilians for the control of the region. It was the worst civil war in Brazilian history, with an estimated toll of 30,000 deaths (Harris 2015).

The Amazon experienced an economic boom circa 1880–1910, centered on rubber. The extraction of the latex from the rubber tree became a very lucrative business, fueled by the then new technology of vulcanization, which allowed for the hardening of rubber and its industrial uses in several applications, such as tires, shoes, domestic utensils and toys.

The rubber barons in Brazil generally used Indigenous labor or migrant workers from the Northeast, consolidating a demographic change in the region (Ribeiro 1995) and its colonization to further extensions of the rainforest, like the state of Acre, a contested territory with Bolivia (Cervo and Bueno 2002). During the boom, there was a wave of impressive constructions in the big cities of the Amazon, such as palaces and the Opera House of Manaus, but the riches of the period did not lead to the socio-economic development of the region.

There was a second rubber boom in the Amazon, short-lived, during the Second World War, when the Japanese occupied Southeast Asia, the rival area of production of the commodity. It happened among concerns of president Getúlio Vargas' administration (1930–1945) with the "March to the West," an expansion of the agricultural frontier to the Mid-West of Brazil, which included some parts of the Amazon, and expeditions to map and pacify Indigenous Peoples in the region (Becker 2009; Bôas and Bôas 2002).

The next big development project in the Amazon was the military dictatorship of 1964–1985. The Armed Forces considered the region part of a geopolitical project of occupation and development of the territory, through big infrastructure initiatives, such as the Transamazônica highway, the Tucuruí hydropower dam, the Carajás mining complex and the industrial park of Manaus. The authoritarian regime stimulated the expansion of agriculture and cattle to the region, often at the expanse of the Indigenous Peoples and riverine communities which inhabited the land (Becker 2009; Valente 2017).

The military dictatorship marked the beginning of large-scale soy plantations and cattle-ranching in the Amazon. Sponsored by the State, farmers and companies started to occupy the rainforest, usually setting it on fire to prepare it for economic exploitation. All that happened before the commodity boom and the rise of China in the twenty-first century, for the goal was to produce for the domestic market—at the time, Brazil was not a major meat exporter and was just starting to develop a modern agribusiness sector (Klein and Luna 2020).

The return of democracy in Brazil in 1985 had strong impacts to the Amazon. Environmental policy began to be something important, with the creation of several public organs at national and local levels (ministries, secretariats, agencies and so on). These civil servants would be important policy-makers in the next decades, especially at the Ministry of Environment and at the Instituto Brasileiro do Meio Ambiente e dos Recursos Naturais Renováveis [Institute of Environment and Renewable Natural Resources]—IBAMA in the Portuguese acronym.

The rising concern with the protection of the Amazon regarding biodiversity and climate change would also be present in Brazilian diplomacy (see Sect. 4.3), with the decisions to host the United Nations Conference on Environment and Development in Rio de Janeiro, in 1992, and to join the UN Framework Convention on Climate Change.

Both trends would be important and contradictory forces shaping the Amazon in the early twenty-first century. On one hand, the expansion of agribusiness and infrastructure investments in the region. On the other hand, the rising power of socioenvironmental movements, often part of international coalitions, acting as check and balances to deforestation and proposing alternative public policies in sustainable development and stronger commitments on climate diplomacy.

The economic frontier in the Amazon is concentrated in the expansion of cattle ranches and soybean plantations, continuing the process initiated by the military in the 1970s. Fifty years, the region was the home of over 40% of the bovine herd of Brazil, with more heads of cattle than people. However, this is far from being a modern economic enterprise, with low-technology, low capital ranches (Bourscheit et al. 2021).

The economic expansion into the region was based on a development model in which fires were used to promote deforestation, wood extraction and get the woods ready to raise cattle. There has been lots of violence and insecurity of property rights, with land grabbing, and conflicts between farmers and local communities (Salles 2021). Indeed, in 2020 77% of murders in Brazil in land conflicts happen in the Amazon (Comissão Pastoral da Terra 2021).

Soybeans came to the Amazon in large-scale in the 1990s, following the growing international demand for the commodity. The farmers usually installed the plantations in land that had already been deforested by wood extraction or cattle-raising, consolidating in a certain way a cycle of the economic occupation of the rainforest (Neher 2020).

National highways have been important for the economic penetration in the rainforest, for the deforestation and the land conflicts are concentrated around 100 km of them (Becker 2009, p. 74). They represent the view of the military regime that infrastructure projects were the best way to integrate the Amazon to the rest of Brazil and to assure the development of its natural resources.

The highway BR-163, which connects Cuiabá to Santarém, is the best example of that. The road cuts through 2,000 km of the Amazon, linking the agribusiness heartland of the Center-West, in the state of Mato Grosso, to the rainforest in Pará. The federal government began its construction in the 1970s, during the dictatorship, and it was the axis around cattle-ranching and soy developed in the region, with the road dotted with farms, grain silos and heavy truck traffic—but also illegal mining, violent conflict over land and deforestation (Nolen 2018).

4.2   China's Impacts in the Amazon

The global commodity boom of the early twenty-first century led to the expansion of Brazil's agribusiness, including the Amazon, which became an economic frontier for soybeans and cattle. China is the biggest export market for these Brazilian products. Correlation is explanation? What are the impacts—positive and negative—of the Chinese in the rainforest?

China's presence in the Amazon comes in three ways: trade, investment and its influence on global regulation on supply chains, to curb deforestation. This section details each one of them.

Chinese influence in the region began by trade, by buying the agricultural and mineral commodities produced in the region. The majority of Brazilian soybean production is for export, and China has been the biggest buyer since the beginning of the twenty-first century (see Chapter 2).

Therefore, Chinese demand has been the most important force in the expansion of soybean in the Amazon. In 2005, there were 1.4 million hectares of plantations in the region. In 2018, 5 million. The area more than tripled in a decade and half (Soendergaard et al. 2021, p. 29).

If China has a direct link with soybean expansion in the Amazon, due to its huge demand, its impact on cattle-ranching is not so big. Although the Chinese are the biggest international market for Brazil's meat, about 80% of the production is for domestic consumption (Bourscheit et al. 2021).

Only 10% of the total production of Brazilian meat goes to China. This is an important detail, for cattle-ranching has been the more serious cause for the deforestation of the Amazon, and so far the initiatives trying to curb it have not been successful, in contrast with better results from soybean farmers (see below).

The high international prices for soybeans, meat and iron ore during the global commodity boom of the 2000s stimulated not only the expansion of the plantations and mining operations, but also the construction of infrastructure. Chinese influence can be seen in the region in the investments in railways and in the heavy traffic in highways such as BR-163 (Chan and Araújo 2020).

Chinese investments in the Amazon began in the 2010s, when big SOEs such as State Grid, China Three Gorges and CCCC started to build infrastructure projects in the region, dealing with energy and transportation. Although just 8% of Chinese FDI in Brazil was in the North region (Cariello 2021), they include some of the most meaningful initiatives, such as the transmission line connecting the Belo Monte dam in the Xingu river to the Southeast, or the Pará railway linking the cities of Marabá and Barcarena.

What led the Chinese to invest in the region? The reasons are the ones discussed in Chapter 3 of this book. China's companies are looking for opportunities in the making access to commodities cheaper and quicker, in order to transport them to Asia at a lower cost. This is especially the case of the investments in railways in the Amazon, which connect areas rich in the production of soybeans, meat and iron ore to fluvial ports from where they can be taken to the Pacific (Abdenur et al. 2021).

Pará is the Amazon state where the Chinese most invested in the Amazon, with projects concentrated in the generation and transmission of electric energy, in the dams in its big rivers, such as Tapajós and Xingu (Cariello 2021). As an economic frontier of the expansion of soybeans and cattle, it is very representative of the trend of China's FDI associated with commodity extraction. It is also the place that concentrated the railways projects that interest the Chinese, such as the Ferrogrão initiative (Abdenur et al. 2021).

However, there are also important trends in the Amazon which defy the stereotype of China's looking only for commodities. In the state of Amazonas, all the investment projects and in manufacturing, with Chinese companies installing factories in the Manaus' Special Economic Zone. Examples include BYD, the electric vehicle firm, Gree, the airconditioning manufacturer, and Traxx, which fabricates motorcycles. This is part of a larger pattern of China's FDI in Brazil in the 2010s showing a bigger attention in the industrial sector, aiming for the Brazilian domestic consumer market (Brito 2017; Cariello 2021).

What are the socioenvironmental impacts of Chinese investments in the Amazon? Did they stimulate conflicts, responses from social movements? Judicial actions from the Brazilian authorities? There is a growing literature very critical, for example, of China's FDI in African countries, highlighting negative impacts such as damage to natural resources and weak labor rules (Chaisse 2019; Lee 2018). Would the same problems apply to the Amazon?

The reality on the ground is quite different from the more critical situations described in the international literature. Brazil has a stronger State, with comprehensive environmental laws, institutions devoted to the protection of social rights, such as the Federal Public Ministry and a dynamic civil society that contests what it perceives to be treats to its wellbeing. It is a complex political framework which requires from Chinese firms' efforts of adaption to the Brazilian conditions.

In the case of the construction of railways, for example, there have been many instances where local communities mobilized against Chinese projects with negative impacts in their lives. In the discussions about the Ferrogrão, a railway that will be parallel to the BR-163, Indigenous Peoples' have been arguing that they do not want the tracks to cross their lands, and sometimes they won legal victories, including decisions by the Supreme Court (Abdenur et al. 2021).

Another example are the infrastructure projects for the generation and transmission of electrical energy, such as the line connecting the Belo Monte dam to the Southeast. They are initiatives that involve a complex web of environmental regulations along several Brazilian states and that require an extensive work of specialized lawyers (Cai 2020).

The more serious conflicts between Chinese companies and local populations in the Amazon happen when there are gaps in Brazilian law, loopholes which make it more difficult to reach the resolution of a conflict. In many situations, this is about the right to prior consultation of Indigenous Peoples and riverine communities about infrastructure projects in their lands.

Brazil signed the Convention 169 of the International Labor Organization which is the global benchmark about the issue, but there is a not national law regulating how the treaty should be applied, and there are many controversies on how to do it. Environmental activists and local communities have accused Chinese companies of not making these consultations in projects such as Ferrogrão or the Teles Pires dam in the Pará state (CICDHA 2021).

Besides the negative impacts from trade and investment, China can also play a positive role in the Amazon as maker or enforcer of international standards of environmental protection, stimulating Brazilian actors to comply with stricter rules against deforestation, carbon emission or other forms of damages to the rainforest. This possibility of Chinese global leadership for the protection of the environment has been a constant issue in the discussions about the country (Finamore 2018; Watts 2010).

It is also part of a bigger pattern concerning China's economic influence in developing nations, especially tropical ones. In the same way that Chinese demand for soybeans or meat is a significant factor in the Amazon, its hunger for palm oil, wood or other commodities is important to countries in Southeast Asia or Africa. Because of that, China has been the target of international campaigns which aim to lobby its authorities to take precautions about the environment in activities such as the lending operations of its development banks (Warmerdam 2021).

Similar concerns are part of the debate on the Chinese influence on the Amazon. As Beijing pays more attention to climate change and adopts more ambitious goals towards carbon-neutrality (see Sect. 4.3), it directs its SOEs to be more engaged in the issue. In Brazil, this happening regarding putting pressure on supply chains, to ensure that they are not involved in illegal deforestation.

The most important Chinese player in these efforts is COFCO, the giant trading company which became a major buyer of Brazilian agribusiness (Chapter 2). In 2020, the firm announced a partnership with the World Bank to track all the soybean that it buys in Brazil until 2023 (COFCO 2020).

The firm's decision is not an exception, but part of local and international trends that began in the 2000s, with growing global concerns with soybean and cattle expansion in the Amazon. The pressure of civil society organizations, public opinion and consumers led Brazilian private sector companies to establish a Soy Moratorium in 2006, vowing to stop deforestation, to do not buy from illegally deforested lands and to track their supply chains. They were joined by the major American and European trading companies. At first, the idea was just to halt deforestation for 10 years, but when this date was reached the moratorium was renewed indefinitely (Soendergaard et al. 2021).

Although it is not an open capital enterprise accountable to shareholders, COFCO is basically behaving in the Amazon in a similar way of Western firms, adapting to a new international scenario where agribusiness has to show commitment to the protection of the environment in order to keep access to global markets and to satisfy consumers concerned with deforestation.

Scholars and NGOs consider the soy moratorium to be a success story, curbing deforestation for soy plantations in the Amazon (Greenpeace 2016; Soendergaard et al. 2021). However, other problems persist and affect COFCO. Mostly, because it is difficult to track a complex web of direct and indirect suppliers (Andreoni et al. 2021; Milhorance and Locatelli 2020).

There is a similar agreement concerning meat, the Beef Moratorium of 2009, result of a negotiation between the Federal Public Ministry, Greenpeace and the major slaughterhouses of Brazil. However, it has not been as successful as the soybean deal, due to the difficult in tracking the supply chain (Bourscheit et al. 2021; Soendergaard et al. 2021).

Although there is no direct Chinese involvement in the Beef Moratorium, the country may eventually become an important player in the pressure to implement it. China is the main international buyer of Brazilian meat, the destination of 10% of the beef production in the country. A similar movement to COFCO's decision concerning soybean would have a huge impact.

Despite the gaps and problems, it is possible to see that China also plays a positive role in curbing deforestation and creating positive economic incentives in the Amazon, in line with initiatives launched by Western and Brazilian actors. In the absence of a global treaty about these issues, pacts between Brazil and a few other countries may have important consequences (Unterstell 2021).

Last but not least, China also has a positive impact stimulating sustainable development projects, due to its demand of products who may support local communities and small farmers in the Amazon. Beyond soybeans and meat, which usually require a large-scale production supply chain, there are other opportunities such as the export of Brazilian nuts or açaí, a regional fruit that became a niche fad with gym users in the United States.

These sustainable products are still quite small in terms of exports, amounting to millions of dollars in a total of over US$100 billion in the bilateral trade, but they have the potential to grow, not only in economic terms of Chinese demands but also as possible objects of joint international cooperation projects towards green economy, as both countries assume stronger commitments in fighting climate change.

4.3   Brazil, China and Climate Diplomacy

In the twenty-first century, China became an important player in climate diplomacy, with big consequences for its relationship with Brazil, itself a major actor due to its control of important biomes such as the Amazon and to its huge biodiversity. Despite the differences in their political systems, both countries share as developing nations a similar trajectory concerning their foreign policy towards the protection of the environment and the rising agenda of curbing global warming.

In the twentieth century, Brazil and China went through an intense developmentalist period where the main goal of the State was to achieve high economic growth and to promote national industrialization and social modernization. However, the environment was not perceived to be a major issue, and it was usually seen as natural resources ready to be exploited for agriculture or industry (Furtado 2005; Shapiro 2001). In both nations, development had a high environmental cost in terms of deforestation, pollution and the extinction of natural species (Watts 2010).

At first, Beijing and Brasilia were hostile to the international agenda of concern with environment that began at the United Nations in the 1970s, with the Stockholm Conference on the Human Environment (1972). Brazilian and Chinese leaders saw environmentalism as a threat to its developmentalist projects (Correa do Lago 2007). In Brazil, the military regime was implementing its economic expansion program in the Amazon. In China, the country was in the final years of Mao Zedong's

Cultural Revolution, and after his death, in the beginning of its opening and reform process. The top priority was growth and other issues could wait.

In Brazil, the redemocratization of the 1980s was a turning point regarding the rise of a local environmentalist movement, and the Amazon played a key role in that. Chico Mendes, the leader of the *seringueiros* (workers in the rubber-extraction in the region) became a world-famous figure and a symbol of the struggles of the new era. From an institutional point of view, the decade was the watershed of creation of public organs dedicated to the protection of the environment. With the passing of the years, they would be the cradle for many career officials who would be important technicians in public policy and climate diplomacy.

A more open approach led Brazil to host in 1992 the UN Conference on Environment and Development, with its landmark discussions such as the Earth Summit, Agenda 21, the Convention on Biodiversity and, especially, the UN Framework Convention on Climate Change (UNFCC), the first and most important diplomatic tool for international cooperation against global warming (Correa do Lago 2007).

The UNFCC recognizes that human action is leading to global warming, and the treaty establishes the commitment to contain it through the reduction of emissions of greenhouse gases. As a framework convention, it is the first step to the creation of additional steps which could deal with specific issues, such as the Kyoto Protocol (in use between 1997–2012) which operationalized goals established in the convention.

In climate changes negotiations, Brazil and China adopted the principle of "common but differentiated responsibilities," enshrined in the article 3 of the convention (UN 1992). The meaning of the expression was that developed countries were considered the primary actors that caused global warming since the Industrial Revolution, due to their emissions of greenhouse gases, and they had binding obligations to reduce them. In contrast, developing nations shared responsibility in facing the problem, but in a lesser degree, and did not have legal commitments to curb their emissions (Harris 1999).

In the 2000s, Brazil progressively started to take more assertive actions regarding the protection of environment, such as the moratoriums on soybean and beef described in Sect. 4.2. In 2005, after record deforestation, the Brazilian government responded with a more effective policy to fight the problem, leading to lower levels of the destruction of the rainforest (Soendergaard et al. 2021).

Deforestation is the main cause of Brazil's carbon emissions. Besides that, the Amazon plays a crucial role as a sink of greenhouse gases, making it a fundamental piece in global efforts to reduce global warming. The preservation of the rainforest became an important part of Brazilian climate diplomacy, a symbol of the country's commitment to the issue.

China was also going to its own transformation in environmental protection in the early twenty-first century. The high costs of its developmental policies became clear, often leading to public health emergencies due to air and water pollution (Watts 2010), desertification, deforestation and similar problems.

In terms of impacts in climate change, the most serious Chinese problem is its energy matrix concentrated in coal. With economic growth, pollution also rose quickly and in 2006 China became the world's biggest carbon emitter. It was increasingly hard to keep defending the thesis of "common but differentiated responsibility", and Beijing was facing stronger pressures from developed countries to assume a broader share of the task of curbing global warming.

This was not something that Chinese authorities were willing to do, and they kept using the argument that per capita emissions were much higher in rich nations than in China. The apex of this conflict was COP15 in Copenhagen, in 2009, when Beijing's refusal to accept binding obligations in reducing its carbon emissions was the main reason for the failure of the negotiators to reach a comprehensive deal (Conrad 2012).

A little before COP15, Brazil, China, India and South Africa band together to create the BASIC, a group dedicated to climate change negotiations. At the time, it was mostly a defensive coalition, of developing nations with a critical view of how Western powers were conducting the discussions. In that sense, BASIC shared many points in common with the BRICS, G77, G20 and similar initiatives (Hallding et al. 2011; Hochsteltler 2012; Qi 2011).

Natalie Unterstell is an environmental researcher and activist who worked for major Brazilian NGOs, such as Instituto Socioambiental, and also served at the federal government as a climate change negotiator. She notes that the choice of Brazilian partners is peculiar: why opt for countries with coal-based energy models, such as China and India, and not other Amazon basin nations, with similar changes as Brazil, such as Colombia or Peru? (Unterstell 2021).

The creation of the BASIC was the result of a process marked by the Brazilian government caution towards mechanisms to mitigate climate change, such as the global market of carbon credit or the REDD + mechanism to fight deforestation. In contrast with the mistrust of Brasília, civil society organizations and local governments in Brazil were much more open to these possibilities (Unterstell 2021).

At the time, China had similar positions, but it changed in the 2010s, especially since the beginning of Xi Jinping's term as president (2012) when the government started to implement a more assertive policy towards the green economy, in what Yifei Li and Judith Shapiro labeled "coercive environmentalism" (Li and Shapiro 2020).

This is a strategy implemented in many fronts. It requires investments in the green economy, stricter laws to regulate pollution and industrial waste, long-term efforts to change the energy matrix from coal to renewable sources (hydroelectric, solar, wind), construction of smart cities and buildings that use less power... These actions are part of a larger trend in Chinese political economic under Xi, the transition from a development model concerned mainly with economic growth to a more balanced view which highlights quality of live, protection of the environment and fighting social issues such as inequality and poverty (Finamore 2018; Li and Shapiro 2020; Andrews-Speed 2019).

In countries like Brazil and the United States, with a democratic federal system, the turn towards more environmental-friendly public policies is complicated by conflicts between the central government and local authorities, with different opinions on the matter. In the context of the late 2010s, that usually meant mayors and governors more concerned with climate change in contrast with presidents Jair Bolsonaro and Donald Trump, which denied that the issue was a problem. In comparison, China's top-down approach resulted in quicker and deeper change (Gallagher and Xuan 2018).

In international negotiations on climate change, the most important consequence of the new Chinese policies was China's acceptance of binding commitments to curb carbon emissions. This led to the Paris Agreement of 2015 at COP21, establishing the goal of keeping world temperatures under 2C above pre-industrial levels, with efforts to maintain them below 1,5C (UN 2015).

There are many reasons that led China to change its historical position on climate change diplomacy. The environmental crisis in the country became a serious domestic problem, with consequences for agriculture and health. The national authority started to implement a new set of public policies to deal with these challenges.

But there is also an international factor: a rising China willing to act as a leader on the fighting against global warming, especially against a hesitating United States, where the subject became part of the cultural wars of partisan polarization. When Trump took out the country from the Paris Agreement, the opportunity became even bigger for Beijing (Gallagher and Xuan 2018; Kopra 2019).

The Brazil of the 2010s and early 2020s was a difficult partner for China in terms of climate diplomacy. The succession of Brazilian political and economic crisis in the period often made public policy erratic. Three presidents had five ministers of the Environment and seven of Foreign Affairs in the ten years since 2011, in the middle of intense ideological struggles between left and right, corruption scandals and recessions.

Brazil was an important player in the negotiations of the Paris Agreement, but as in the United States the election of a president who denied that climate change was happening ended this key role. Brazilian voter elected Jair Bolsonaro in 2018 as part of a general mood of rejection of the traditional political class (see Chapter 5).

Although Bolsonaro did not take Brazil out of the Paris agreement, his government stopped international cooperation against global warming, and Amazon deforestation rates rose to record levels. The support base of the president included many ranchers and farmers who saw strict environmental protection as an obstacle to development. Bolsonaro himself criticized what the defined as the "industry of [environmental] fines," claiming that the State should stop to penalize entrepreneurs who wanted to develop Brazil.

As a results of the new ideological orientation of the Brazilian government, the country stopped to play a leadership role in climate change negotiations under the Bolsonaro administration. In many ways, it was a reversal to the positions of the 1970s, when the military regime considered the Amazon from the perspective of economic resources to be exploited for economic growth. However, Brazil's society—and the world—had changed a lot, and the president had less room for maneuver.

Brazil faced strong pressures from Western governments and companies because of Amazon's deforestation, with firms refusing to buy Brazilian agribusiness products or recommending investor to take the money out of the sector. It was a repetition, in a harsher way, of the soybean and beef moratorium campaigns of the 2000s.

Diplomatic relations with the European Union became more complicated because of the issue, and the same happened with the United States in 2021, after the election of Joseph Biden as president, when the American government returned to the Paris Agreement and highlighted the importance of climate change. There was perplexity in the White House about how to deal with Bolsonaro, even if many officials perceived him as an important player in dealing with China's rising influence in Latin America (Winter 2021).

But Beijing's reaction was different. The Chinese government adopted a non-interference posture towards Bolsonaro's environmental policy, refusing to criticize the Brazilian president on the issue. The gesture was an attempt to pacify the Brazilian administration in face of concerns with the strategic partnership (see Chapter 5).

Moreover, China is playing the long game in Brazil. Beijing bet on green economy, eco-development and climate change goes many years in future, and it knows that the Amazon will be an important of its relationship with its South American partner, both during and after Bolsonaro's stay in the presidency.

In the next generation, China plans to march to carbon-neutrality, and to reach this goal it will invest in renewable energy, both at home and abroad, to finance sustainable development projects, and to implement stricter certification protocols to the agricultural products it buys from Brazil. All these initiatives pose several challenges but many opportunities for Brazilians, as they take the strategic partnership with China to a new level in the twenty-first century.

REFERENCES

Abdenur, Adriana, Folly, Maiara, and Santoro, Maurício. *What Railway Deals Taught Chinese and Brazilians in the Amazon*. Washington: Carnegie Endowment for International Peace, 2021.

Andreoni, Manuela, Tabuchi, Hiroko, and Sun, Alberto. "How Americans' Appetite for Leather in Luxury SUVs Worsens Amazon Deforestation." *New York Times*, November 17th, 2021.

Andrews-Speed, Philip. *China as a Global Clean Energy Champion: Lifting the Veil*. London: Palgrave, 2019.

Becker, Bertha K. *Amazônia, geopolítica na virada do III milênio*. Rio de Janeiro: Garamond, 2009.

Bôas, Orlando Villas and Bôas, Cláudio Villas. *A Marcha para o Oeste: a epopeia da expedição Roncador-Xingu*. São Paulo: Companhia das Letras, 2002.

Bourscheit, Aldem et alli. *Sob a Pata do Boi: como a Amazônia vira pasto*. Rio de Janeiro: Associação O Eco, 2021.

Brito, Cleiton Ferreira Maciel. "Made in China - Produzido no Polo Industrial da Zona Franca de Manaus: o trabalho nas fábricas chinesas." PhD dissertation. Federal University of São Carlos, 2017.

Cai, Hongxiang. "Nove anos de trabalhos duros no Brasil: a história de crescimento da State Grid Corporation no Brasil." In: Zhou Zhiwei e Wu Changsheng (orgs) *Histórias de Amizade entre China e Brasil*. Beijing: China International Press, 2020.

Cariello, Túlio. *Investimentos Chineses no Brasil: histórico, tendências e desafios globais (2007-2020)*. Rio de Janeiro: Conselho Empresarial Brasil-China, 2021.

Cervo, Amado and Bueno, Clodoaldo. *História da Política Exterior do Brasil*. Brasília: Editora da Universidade de Brasília, 2002.

Chaisse, Julien. (org). *China's International Investment Strategy: Bilateral, Regional, and Global Law and Policy*. Oxford: Oxford University Press, 2019.

Chan, Melissa and Araújo, Heriberto. "China Wants Food. Brazil Pays the Price." *The Atlantic*, February 15, 2020.

COFCO. "COFCO International aims for full traceability of all directly sourced soy across Brazil by 2023." Beijing, COFCO, July 2nd 2020. Available at https://www.cofcointernational.com/stories/cofco-international-aims-for-full-traceability-of-all-directly-sourced-soy-across-brazil-by-2023/

Colectivo sobre Financiamiento e Inversiones Chinas, Derechos Humanos y Ambiente (CICDHA). *Tercer Ciclo de la Evaluación Periódica Universal de la República Popular de China desde Sociedad Civil*. CICDHA, 2021.

Comissão Pastoral da Terra, "Conflitos no Campo Brasil 2020." Goiânia: Centro de Documentação Dom Tomás Balduíno, 2021.

Conrad, Bjorn. "China in Copenhagen: Reconciling the "Beijing Climate Revolution" and the "Copenhagen Climate Obstinacy." *The China Quarterly*, Volume 210, 2012.

Correa do Lago, André. *Estocolmo, Rio, Joanesburgo: o Brasil e as três conferências ambientais das Nações Unidas*. Brasília: Funag, 2007.

Estenssoro Saavedra, Fernando. *La Geopolítica Ambiental del Siglo XXI: los desafíos para América Latina*. Santiago: RIL Editores, 2019.

Finamore, Barbara. *Will China Save the Planet?* Cambridge: Polity Press, 2018.

Furtado, Celso. *O Mito do Desenvolvimento Econômico*. São Paulo: Paz e Terra, 2005.

Gallagher, Kelly Sims and Xuan, Xiaowei. *Titans of the Climate: Explaining Policy Process in the United States and China*. Cambridge: MIT Press, 2018.

Greenpeace. "10 Years Ago the Amazon Was Being Bulldozed for Soy—Then Everything Changed." May 22, 2016. Available at https://www.greenpeace.org/usa/victories/amazon-rainforest-deforestation-soy-moratorium-success/

Hallding, Karl et al. *Together Alone: Brazil, South Africa, India, China (BASIC) and the Climate Change Conundrum*. Stockholm: Stockholm Environment Institute, 2011.

Harris, Mark. *Rebellion on the Amazon: the Cabanagem, Race, and Popular Culture in the North of Brazil, 1798–1840*. Cambridge: Cambridge University Press, 2015.

Harris, Paul. "Common But Differentiated Responsibility: The Kyoto Protocol and United States Policy." *NYU Environmental Law Journal*, Volume 27, 1999.

Hochsteltler, Kathryn Ann. "The G-77, BASIC, and Global Climate Governance: A New Era in Multilateral Environmental Negotiations." *Revista Brasileira de Política Internacional*, Volume 55, 2012.

Klein, Hebert and Luna, Francisco. *Alimentando o mundo: o surgimento da moderna economia agrícola no Brasil*. Rio de Janeiro: FGV, 2020.

Kopra, Sanna. *China and Great Power Responsibility for Climate Change*. London: Routledge, 2019.

Lee, Kwan Ching. *The Specter of Global China: Politics, Labor, and Foreign Investment in Africa*. Chicago: University of Chicago Press, 2018.

Li, Yifei e Shapiro, Judith. *China Goes Green: Coercive Environmentalism for a Troubled Planet*. Cambridge: Polity, 2020.

Milhorance, Flavia and Locatelli, Piero. "Questions Persist over Giant Chinese Soy Trader's Track and Trace Plan." *Diálogo Chino*. October 9th, 2020.

Neher, Clarissa. "O papel de gado e soja no ciclo de desmatamento." *Deutshe Welle*, April 24th, 2020.

Nolen, Stephanie. "Highway of Riches, Road to Ruin." *The Globe and Mail*, January 26th 2018.

Pereira, Joana Castro and Viola, Eduardo. *Climate Change and Biodiversity Governance in the Amazon*. London: Routledge, 2021.

Qi, Xinran. "The Rise of BASIC in UN Climate Change Negotiations." *South African Journal of International Affairs*, Volume 18, Issue 3, 2011.

Ribeiro, Darcy. *O Povo Brasileiro: a formação e o sentido do Brasil*. São Paulo: Companhia das Letras, 1995.

Salles, João Moreira. "Arrabalde: Parte III_ a fronteira é um país estrangeiro." *Piauí*, Edition 172, January 2021.

Shapiro, Judith. *Mao's War Against Nature: Politics and the Environment in Revolutionary China*. Cambridge: Cambridge University Press, 2001.

Soendergaard, Neil, Dias de Sá, Camila, Jank, Marcos, and Gilio, Leandro. *Decoupling Soy and Beef from Illegal Amazon Deforestation: Brazilian private Sector Initiatives*. Rio de Janeiro: CEBRI/Insper Agro Global, 2021.

Souza, Marcio. *História da Amazônia: do período pré-colombiano aos desafios do século XXI*. Rio de Janeiro: Record, 2019.

United Nations. *Paris Agreement*. Paris: 2015.

———. *United Nations Framework Convention on Climate Change*. 1992.

Unterstell, Natalie. Interview to the author. Rio de Janeiro, December 17th, 2021.

Valente, Rubens. *Os Fuzis e as Flechas*. São Paulo: Companhia das Letras, 2017.

Warmerdam, Ward. Chinese banks' forest-risk financing: financial flows and client risks. São Francisco: Forests & Finance, 2021.

Watts, Jonanthan. *When a Billion Chinese Jump: how China will save mankind – or destroy it*. New York: Scribner, 2010.

Winter, Brian. "The Silent Partner. Biden Wants Distance from Bolsonaro—But also Wants Brazil Aligned Against China." *Piaui*. Edition 180, September 2021.

Weinstein, Barbara. *The Amazon Rubber Boom, 1850-1920*. Stanford: Stanford University Press, 1982.

CHAPTER 5

The Dragon and the Captain: China in the Perspective of Brazil's Nationalist Right

The 2000s were in retrospect a golden age to Sino-Brazilian relations, with the global commodities boom consolidating the strategic partnership that was designed ten years before. But the decade of 2010 presented a different context. Brazil suffered a series of economic recessions and political crisis that led to rise of new ideological forces of the nationalist right which were up to then on the fringes of the system. These new groups reached power with a hostile vision of China and the desire to re-establish a preferential relationship with the United States, trying to re-create the alliance with Washington that was an important part of the Brazilian foreign policy in the first half of the twentieth century.

This chapter analyzes how the Brazilian nationalist right rose to the presidency and how it views China and influences the making of the foreign policy towards Beijing. The first section explains how this political group grew among the crises of the 2010s and won Brazil's 2018 presidential election.

The following section identifies the three lines of criticism that the nationalist right has on China: economic policy, national security and cultural identity. The first is concerned about protecting Brazilian industry and promoting fair trade; the second is worried about Chinese control of natural resources and key infrastructure in the country, and the third advocates Brazil's partnership with the Western powers and the defense

© The Author(s), under exclusive license to Springer Nature Singapore Pte Ltd. 2022
M. Santoro, *Brazil–China Relations in the 21st Century*,
https://doi.org/10.1007/978-981-19-0353-3_5

of Christian heritage. It has many points in common with the alt-right in the United States or with national-populist movements in Europe.

The third section discusses the role of the nationalist right in the making of Brazil's foreign policy towards China. It argues that this group disputes power and influence with another interest groups with a more positive view of the Chinese, such as the agribusiness. However, they introduced tensions in the strategic partnership with Beijing, changing the dynamic of the bilateral relation.

The last section addresses the impact of the coronavirus pandemic in Sino-Brazilian relations, claiming that the outbreak of Covid-19 made Brazil realize how dependent the country is on China, due to economic needs and medical assistance, but it also stimulated anti-Chinese feeling among the population, often instigated by the leaders of the nationalist right.

5.1   The Rise of the Nationalist Right in Brazil

In 2018, the former Army captain Jair Bolsonaro won the presidential election in Brazil. A backbencher in Congress for almost 30 years, he rose quickly in Brazilian politics during the crises of the 2010s. His victory was a powerful symbol of the rejection of the political establishment by voters tired of recessions and corruption scandals. He is the first Brazilian president since the 1970s to take office criticizing China as a negative influence for the country.

Bolsonaro's election was part of a larger trend concerning the crisis of the Brazilian democracy under construction since 1985. In the beginning of that cycle, the national right was weak, due to its association to the two decades long military dictatorship which ended in deep economic crisis (see Chapter 1). The conservative parties which supported the military regime reinvented themselves around a liberal economic agenda, supporting reforms such as lowering tariffs, promoting privatization and inserting Brazil in a more open and integrated global economy (Mainwaring et al. 2000).

The foreign policy of the military regime promoted Brazil as a middle-power, searching for influence in the Third World and autonomy in developing science and technology, especially in atomic power (Cervo and Bueno 2002; Vizentini 1998). In the 1990s, the Brazilian presidents changed that orientation and the country joined international regimes forbidding weapons of mass destruction (biological, chemical, nuclear) and protecting human rights. The rationale was establishing Brasília as a credible, rule-abiding partner in the new global order, to attract foreign trade and investment (Cervo and Bueno 2002; Vigevani et al. 2003). Right-wing nationalist politicians were relegated to the fringe of the public debate, often seemed as outdated or even comical figures whose time has passed.

The political scenario changed in the 2010s. The economic situation started to worsen after the global financial crisis of 2008, turning into the biggest recession of Brazil modern history in 2014–2016, when GDP fell by 8%. The Operation Car Wash of the Federal Police revealed a massive corruption scandal in Petrobras, the giant State-controlled oil company, which involved all the major political parties. There were massive demonstrations against the government and president Dilma Rousseff, who as impeached and replaced by her vice-president Michel Temer, who faced corruption charges himself. The economy grew little more than 1% per year (Safatle et al. 2016).

In the context of crisis and general mistrust in politicians and institutions, the nationalist right staged a comeback with an anti-left rhetoric that blamed Brazil's presidents since the redemocratization for the country's troubles and promised to make the nation great again. The contrast was with the nostalgia for the dictatorship, when growth rates were high, up to 10% per year. The nationalist right also presented a conservative agenda critical the social changes of the last decade, of ethnical and sexual minorities, feminist groups, artists and intellectuals. There was a longing for traditional models of family and gender roles. There were many points in common with Donald Trump in the United States and the national-populist right in Europe, and an increasing level of international cooperation and dialogue among themselves (Sedgwick 2019; Teitelbaum 2020).

The most important politician of the new nationalist right in Brazil is Bolsonaro. Born in low-middle class family in a small town in São Paulo, he joined the Army during the dictatorship and started his political career in the late 1980s. When serving as captain, he organized illegal demonstrations in support of pay rise for the troops and made public criticism in the press of civilian politicians. A military court ordered his retirement from the Armed Forces, but he profited from the episode to launch a successful electoral campaign to the City Council of Rio de Janeiro. After that, he served several terms in Congress, where he was basically a trade union leader for low-ranking soldiers and police officers (Maklouf Carvalho 2019; Pires 2020).

Bolsonaro's popularity started to rise in the mid-2010s. During the many crises of the decade, he presented himself as an outsider who was never trusted by the country's political establishment, a common man mocked by a corrupt elite. The presidential election of 2018 was marked the trial and conviction of former president Lula, under corruption charges, and by an assassination attempt on Bolsonaro, who was stabbed by a deranged man. The former Army captain won the campaign without the support of major political parties and with almost no TV time, using mostly social media to spread his slogans and to mobilize his supporters (Winter, 2018).

5.2   CHINA IN BRAZIL'S NATIONALIST RIGHT WORLDVIEW

Bolsonaro was the first Brazilian president since the establishment of diplomatic ties with the People's Republic of China to criticize the country, presenting it as a bad influence to Brazil. He broke a foreign policy consensus of 45 years and reintroduced in the ideological debate an anti-communist rhetoric which seemed to be part of the past, of the Cold War discussions.

During the 2018 presidential campaign, Bolsonaro and his three eldest sons—all of them are also politicians—visited Taiwan. They were the first important Brazilian officials to do so. The trip to the island was part of an East Asian tour that included Japan and South Korea, but left out the biggest trade partner of Brazil—China. In Taipei, Bolsonaro called Taiwan "a country" and said that it was a synthesis of the best that Americans and Japanese have to offer (Santoro 2018).

The visit to Taiwan made the Chinese embassy in Brazil do something without precedents in the bilateral diplomatic history: it sent a letter to each member of the Brazilian Congress stating the importance of the "One China" policy that Brasília follows since the diplomatic recognition of the People's Republic in 1974. There was a concern among the Chinese diplomats that Bolsonaro could change that if he was elected president.

The candidate's position on the issue was not clear, for his campaign manifesto was a very simple document, written in bullets points, looking more like a power point presentation than a comprehensive ideological platform. It had just one page about international affairs, where Bolsonaro praised the United States, Israel and Italy (then under a coalition which included the populist Five Star Movement) and criticized the left-wing governments of Latin America. There was no mention about China (Bolsonaro 2018).

His political line towards Beijing became clear when he won the election and announced his minister of Foreign Affairs. He chose career diplomat Ernesto Araújo, a newly promoted ambassador who wrote a blog called "Metapolitics," aligned with alt-right and populist agendas. In an article to a journal published by the ministry, he supported Trump and argued that Western countries (including in his view, Brazil) should band together to defend their Christian and democratic heritage in the face of a rising China, that he considered a threat (Araújo 2017).

These were uncommon position among Brazilian diplomats, who since the 1970s recognized in China an important partner for Brazil, and over the decades had helped to build BRICS, BASIC, the G20 and other initiatives close to Beijing. But ambassador Araújo was not alone—he was part of a larger trend of the return of conservative ideas to the mainstream of Brazilian political debate (Dieguez 2019).

The nationalist right is not a homogenous group, it can be classified in different currents of thought. Araújo is part of a group whose self-description is "anti-globalist," a term they took from the new American populist right. They claim to not oppose globalization itself, but what they perceive as an ideological liberal plot to use this process to weaken the national State and to promote left-wing values (Teitelbaum 2020).

The most important reference for the anti-globalist is Olavo de Carvalho, a writer and social media influencer who became a mentor to this new generation of conservative and populist activists in Brazil. Carvalho is a harsh critic of the left and of the intellectual establishment. Carvalho has been living in the United States for many years, and he introduced to his audience and students many thinkers of the alt-right and build bridges with populist leaders such as Steve Bannon (Sedgwick 2019).

Although Carvalho never joined the Bolsonaro administration, he had several former students and disciples in the government, in important offices: Araújo, two of the ministers of Education, one of the president's sons, congressman Eduardo Bolsonaro, and a special international advisor to Bolsonaro, Filipe Martins. They were the frontline of the criticism against China in Brazil's foreign policy, advocating a rupture of the strategic partnership and closer relations to the United States.

The second important group in Brazil nationalist right are the Armed Forces. The military were very present in the Bolsonaro administration, more than in any other Brazilian government since the return of the democracy. Generals, Admirals and Air Force senior officers form more than one third of the cabinet and around 6,000 officers serve in other top posts, such as chairmen of public companies and state agencies or high rank staff at the ministries (Agostini 2020).

They military officers usually have a foreign policy view which is more conservative that the diplomatic status quo of the last decades, but that do not want to destroy the consensus forged by diplomats and politicians. Many of the generals in the Bolsonaro administration served in UN peace operations, especially in Haiti, and understand the importance of international institutions, in contrast with the hostile view towards them of the anti-globalists. They are also more open to free trade and globalization (Santoro 2019, April 1).

Concerning China, they usually support the strategic partnership, and they realize how crucial the Chinese market is to the Brazilian agribusiness, oil and mining companies. However, they are sometimes worried by the Communist Party and by what they perceive to be attempts of ideological proselytism of Beijing.

Coronel Paulo Gomes Filho is a retired officer from the Brazilian Army who got a master degree from the National Defense University in Beijing. Through his blog and courses, he became an important analyst of Chinese policy. Gomes Filho says that the military are disturbed by the fact that China's People's Liberation Army (PLA) answers to the Communist Party, and not to State. The role of the political commissars in the PRC's Armed Forces is strange to officers trained in the Western tradition of unified command (Gomes Filho 2021).

However, he notices that there are many points in common of the PLA with other Armies and that military officers from anywhere can appreciate its modernization in the last decades and understand its improvements. Gomes Filho highlights the Chinese effort to play a global role, offering military courses in several languages and receiving soldiers from different regions (Gomes Filho 2021).

The Brazilian military leaders are also concerned about Chinese investment in key infrastructure in Brazil. However, these negative views can also be balanced by the admiration regarding China's achievements in economic development, and the perception that the country has important lessons to teach (Castro 2021).

The nationalist right has three main lines of criticism against China: economic policy, national security and cultural identity. The first is a common argument in disputes with Beijing, the latter two, especially the third one, are more peculiar of this political line of thinking.

The criticism about economic policy blames China for bad practices and considers it responsible for many of Brazil's troubles. The argument is that Chinese dumping, weak labor/environmental protections, government subsidies and other actions are unfair trade and affect in a negative way Brazilian companies, diminishing their competitiveness and promoting deindustrialization. This has been an important part of Brazil's trade debate on China, fueling protectionism demands (see Chapter 2).

The national security criticism is a concern that Chinese investments in Brazil are leaving Beijing in charge of strategic natural resources and key infrastructure in energy and telecommunication. The most famous statement from Bolsonaro on the issue is his line that: "China is not buying in Brazil. China is buying Brazil" (Senra 2019).

This is a view often expressed by officers in the Armed Forces. The military regime of 1964–1985 had a nationalist economic policy, based on promoting Brazilian industrialization through State action and the protection of the domestic market and often restricting or forbidding foreign investment in many sectors, such as oil or telecommunications (Abreu 2020). The liberal reforms of the 1990s opened many sectors to FDI, privatized SOEs and did not create mechanisms for limiting the presence of firms from other countries on the bases of the ideology of their governments (see Chapter 3). For many of Brazil's military leaders, this a gap in the legislation that became clear when China started to invest heavily in the country, in the 2010s.

The criticism of cultural identity is specific of the nationalist right, especially of its anti-globalist current. This line of argumentation states that the rise of China is a threat to Western civilization due to its political system and values, and that Brazil should seek a diplomatic rapprochement with the United States to counter the ascension of Beijing (Araújo 2017).

Ambassador Araújo was the most outspoken defender of this view in his tenure as minister of Foreign Affairs (2019–2021). He opposed multilateral deals on climate change, such as the 2015 Paris Agreement, claiming that they were dogma that favored China. He said that Brazil should be cautions of Beijing's worldview: "We want to sell soy and iron ore, but we're not going to sell our soul" (Lapper 2019).

Eduardo Bolsonaro, the president's son, compared the Sino-Brazilian strategic partnership with the Brazilian diplomatic agreements with Hitler's Germany in the 1930s, under president Getúlio Vargas (Lapper 2019).

Although the criticisms on economic policy and national security have been part of the Brazilian debate on how to deal with China, the cultural identity concerns were on the fringe of the serious discussions until the election of Bolsonaro. The mainstream consensus on the diplomatic community on China was the support of the strategic partnership, the common positions on multilateral organizations and a pragmatic approach regarding the Chinese political system, based on non-interference in their domestic issues (Oliveira 2004).

5.3   The Nationalist Right in the Making of Foreign Policy Towards China

The nationalist right is an important group in the political base of the Bolsonaro administration, but it is not alone in the making of the foreign policy towards China. There are several conflicts with other influential actors, such as the technocrats at the ministries of Foreign Affairs, Economy and Agriculture, who favor a more traditional approach in maintaining good relations with Beijing.

The nationalist right itself is divided between anti-globalist and the military officers. Anti-globalists are usually younger and somewhat of outsiders. They are influential on social media but tend to be disregarded by the political establishment. Even ambassador Araújo was never the head of a Brazilian diplomatic mission, nor had any high office until the president chose him as minister.

The conflicts between the anti-globalists and military officers in the Bolsonaro administration have been strong, with public disagreements and offenses concerning China. Vice-president Hamilton Mourão, a retired Army general, consolidated himself as the most important leader for the interest groups searching for a pragmatic relationship with Beijing. As president of Cosban, the bilateral high-level commission, he highlighted the importance of the Chinese trade and investments (including

Huawei) and advocated that Brazil should not take sides in the Sino-American disputes (Santoro, 2019, May 26).

Other important players are the economic technocrats, who are usually allies of the military officers against the anti-globalists. The officials at the Ministry of Infrastructure see Chinese investments as a key opportunity for the Brazilian public–private partnership program, aimed at overcoming the infrastructure bottleneck, and kept their policy of attracting these resources to major projects, such as railways (see Chapter 3).

During the first year of his administration (2019), Bolsonaro generally conducted a pragmatic diplomacy towards China, along the lines of the strategic partnership. He and general Mourão made successful visits to the country and stressed the importance of trade and investment. Chinese SOEs were politically important in the November 2019 pre-salt oil auction—if not for their apport, only the Brazilian Petrobras would have taken part in the operation, due to problems in the rules of the operation (Rosa 2019).

However, the anti-China trend in the administration introduced tensions in the strategic partnership. Anti-globalists generated lot of headlines, because of their strong statements and by their use of social media, even if their actual foreign policy influence was disputed. The role of the president was ambivalent, for people very close to Bolsonaro, such as his son Eduardo, often criticized China in a harsh way, without being reprehended by him.

The tensions did not escalate into a major change of foreign policy, but increased mistrust in Brasília-Beijing relations among a complex international scenario of the Sino-American trade war and Brazil own efforts to overcome the recession and low-growth years of the 2010s.

The outbreak of the coronavirus pandemic in 2020 add another layer of conflict to that precarious equilibrium between the groups that clashed for the control of foreign policy in the Bolsonaro administration.

5.4   The Sino-Brazilian Relations and the Coronavirus Pandemic

The pandemic was a catalyzer to the relations between Brazil and China, reinforcing patterns and issues that have been growing in the last years. The two most important among them: it increased the important of the Chinese market for Brazilians, in a period of global crisis, but at the same time it strengthened criticism of Beijing in the South American country (Santoro 2021). At the official level, the tensions that have been building between both governments since the beginning of the Bolsonaro administration rose to the front lines and led to fall of the minister of Foreign Affairs and to a change in the diplomacy.

The first impact on Sino-Brazilian relations was the bilateral trade. During 2020, Brazil's exports fell 5,4% in comparison to the previous year, following the global economic slowdown. However, the sells to China increased 7%, a little more than a third of Brazilian global sales. The good performance was due to the Chinese capacity of keep its GDP growth even after the coronavirus outbreak. The trade between both countries broke records and achieved US$102.4 billion. As it has been the pattern since the global commodity boom of the 2000s, Brazilian exports to China were concentrated in soybeans, iron ore and oil.[1]

These results were a strong contrast with the exchanges between Brazil and its other major economic partners. The exports to the United States, Argentina and the European Union fell in 2020, respectively, by −27.7, −13.3 and −7.8%.[2] The American numbers were especially significant, both by the scale of the decline and by the efforts of the Bolsonaro administration to establish a close partnership with Trump, arguing that it would be the key to the prosperity of Brazil's foreign trade.

As in many other countries, the pandemic also made Brazilians realize how much they depend on China for medical supplies. Brazil became an important part of Chinese mask diplomacy.

China's mask diplomacy also created important opportunities for paradiplomacy. State governors who wanted to establish good relations with Beijing negotiated their own deals on international health cooperation, bypassing president Bolsonaro and the national authorities in Brasília. The two more important cases were São Paulo and Maranhão.

São Paulo is the richest state in Brazil and was a pioneer in paradiplomacy in the country, with a focus on attracting foreign trade and investment. These were the reasons that led its governor to open an office of its investment agency, InvesteSP, in Shanghai, in 2019. With the pandemic, it also became a very important tool for vaccine diplomacy.

---

[1] Data from the Brazilian Ministry of Economy, http://comexstat.mdic.gov.br/pt/comex-vis. Access September 2021.

[2] Idem.

Through its work, InvesteSP contacted the Chinese pharmaceutical company Sinopharm and established a partnership with Butantan Institute, a state scientific research center of global reputation. Together they started to produce the Coronavac vaccine, which in January 2021 became the first to be distributed to the Brazilian people.

The partnership was perhaps the most ambitious action of paradiplomacy in Brazil. It was part not only of the context of the pandemic, but also of the tensions between the president and the Chinese authorities, and how these problems created opportunities to state governors. João Doria, the governor of São Paulo, was a former ally turned rival of Bolsonaro, who sometimes seemed a possible presidential candidate in Brazil. Being the first politician to offer vaccines against the coronavirus was an important step in his political career.

These actions also made Doria a target of Bolsonaro criticism. The president called Coronavac "Vachina," playing with the words "vaccine" (vacina, in Portuguese) and China, and advising the population not to take it. The advice carried weight among Brazilians and many refused the Coronavac, especially more educated and richer individuals, which were more likely to support the president and to have a more critical view of Beijing, preferring to look for American or European vaccines.

Maranhão is another important case of paradiplomacy in the pandemic. The state is one of the poorest in the country and already a public health system with many problems before the pandemic. After the coronavirus outbreak, it suffered from an acute scarcity of ventilators. It tried to buy them in partnership with other Brazilian states, but the cargo of 600 units was apprehended in the Miami airport, on its transit from China to Brazil.

Governor Flávio Dino and his team looked for support from the federal government, but received only vague advice. Instead, they negotiated a partnership with the private sector, making deals with companies such as the mining giant Vale and the retail chain Mateus chain. Both were used to buy in China and had ample experience of the complex logistics of the country (William 2021).

With the help of these private companies, the government of Maranhão was able to buy 107 ventilators in China, and take them to Brazil via Ethiopian Airlines, an airline companies which uses transportation hubs in Africa—there was not the risk of the cargo being confiscated in the United States by American authorities (William 2021). If São Paulo has been building its paradiplomacy capacities in China for some time, Maranhão had to improvise to respond to a public health emergency.

The governors of the two states have very different political affiliations. Doria is a businessman who ran for office with a market-friendly and conservative platform. Dino is a former judge with a career in left-wing movements—during the pandemic he switched from the Brazilian Communist Party to the socialists. But they both understood how important a good relationship with Beijing would be in order to achieve public health results in the pandemic.

However, the rising importance of China to Brazil was also accompanied by a strong anti-Chinese feeling, stimulated by the rhetoric of the president and his political allies, including his son, congressman Eduardo Bolsonaro, and the ministers of Education and Foreign Affairs. They used social media to post messages criticizing China's Communist Party and blaming it for the coronavirus. The president himself even described the pandemic as a type of "chemical warfare" (Santoro 2021).

This political discourse had a strong impact in a population scared by the pandemic and confused by the lack of a proper public health response—by the end of 2021 Brazil had more than 600,000 confirmed deaths by Covid-19. Many Brazilians endorsed anti-China statements. One survey found that 34% had a positive view of the Asian country and 44%, a negative one. The more critical views correlated strongly with support for Bolsonaro, but they were widespread among all social groups (Traumann 2021).

Supporters of the president organized demonstrations against China in front of the country's diplomatic representations in Brasília, São Paulo and Rio de Janeiro. In September 2021, a man threw a homemade bomb at the Chinese consulate in Rio. The police did not discover who was responsible for the attack.

Although there were not meaningful incidents of street violence against Asian-Brazilians (in comparison with the United States, e.g.), xenophobia also rose in Brazil, with online harassment against Chinese immigrants and their descendants in the country. Sometimes, Japanese and Korean were also the target of this kind of racism. Aggressors linked China with the coronavirus, attacked its culture and traditions and threatened Chinese to leave Brazil and go back home.

Chinese diplomats in Brazil reacted to this scenario in a more assertive way than in the past. Instead of backstage and discreet work with politicians and government officials, they went to the press and to the social media to respond to critics and to present China's perspective, often with personal criticism of Brazilian rulers or of Western diplomats.

The Chinese ambassador in Brasília, Yang Wanming, became a strong presence in Brazil's Twitter, with over 85,000 followers. His posts on vaccines and on the need of scientific knowledge to fight the pandemic were often shared by the opposition of Bolsonaro. He often used humor to criticize the actions of the president (Frazão 2020).

China's consul in Rio de Janeiro, Li Yang, published several Op-Eds on Sino-Brazilian relations. In one of them, he responded to Eduardo Bolsonaro, the president's son, who called the coronavirus "the Chinese virus": "Are you so naïve and ignorant? Did the United States brainwashed you?"(Li 2020).

This type of exchange between foreign diplomats and Brazilian politicians is without precedent, and part of the new "Wolf Warrior" Chinese diplomacy of the Xi Jinping years (Martin 2021). This global trend was reinforced in Brazil due to China's will to respond to the criticism of the Bolsonaro administration, and perhaps because of the perception that it could do so, for the economic dependence of Brazilians of the Chinese market is so big that it gives more room for Beijing to maneuver. Without the fear, for example, that the national government will declare its diplomats *persona non grata* and expel them from the country.

The troubled relationship with China was one of reasons that led to the fall of the minister of Foreign Affairs, ambassador Ernesto Araújo—together with environmental conflicts with the United States concerning the Amazon. There were several conflicts between him and the Senate, with strong criticism especially from senators from the big agribusiness states from the Center-West, such as Kátia Abreu, a soybean farmer and the chairwoman of the Committee on Foreign Affairs.

It was the first time in Brazil's diplomatic history that China played a major role in the change of a minister of Foreign Affairs. Probably, it won't be the last. Araújo was replaced by another career diplomat, ambassador Carlos França, with a more discreet and low-profile rhetoric. Regarding Beijing, he basically repeated the traditional statements of the strategic partnership, moving away from the anti-communist discourse of his predecessor.

The nationalist right returned to power in Brazil in the wave of the crisis of the 2010s after a hiatus of more than 30 years. In the new democracy, it was traditionally associated with the military dictatorship and perceived as outdated in face of conservative parties who were trying to adapt themselves to a new context of globalization.

The corruption scandals, economic recession and political instability of the current decade discredited Brazilian main parties and opened the way to outsiders and backbenchers and led to the victory of Bolsonaro in the 2018 elections. The president shares many of the values and worldview of the nationalist right in foreign policy, such as the priority of the relations with the United States and a critical view of China.

These criticisms are basically divided along three lines: economy policy, pointing to how Brazilian industry loses from unfair competition from China; national security, highlighting concerns about Chinese control of key natural resources and infrastructure; and cultural identity, stressing Brazil's ties with the Western nations and the need to seek out a Christian heritage in diplomacy.

The nationalist right is divided in two contending groups. One, more moderate and closer to traditional conservatives, is the senior military officers in the Bolsonaro administration. The other is the anti-globalist faction, which has many similar points with the new conservative and populist movements in the United States and Europe. It breaks the consensus of the foreign policy elites and clashes with several organized interests who benefit from Chinese trade and investments.

The new nationalist right rise is important to Brazilian diplomacy. It does not set the agenda, but it influences the relationship with China, sometimes creating frictions. A pragmatic approach, more open to economic partnership with Beijing, has been in course, based upon an alliance between the military officers and technocrats. In practice many of their criticism of the Chinese have been sidelined in face of the difficult economic situation of Brazil, and it will probably be so in the near post-pandemic future, when Asia's markets will be even more important for Brazilian products.

References

Abreu, Marcelo de Paiva (ed) *A Ordem do Progresso: dois séculos de política econômica no Brasil*. São Paulo: Editora GEN LTC, 2020.

Agostini, Renata. "Número de militares em cargos civis cresce e passa de 6 mil no governo Bolsonaro." *CNN Brasil*, July 17, 2020.

Araújo, Ernesto. Trump e o Ocidente. *Cadernos de Política Exterior*. Ano III. Número 6. 2º semestre 2017.

Bolsonaro, Jair. *O Caminho da Prosperidade: proposta de plano de governo*, 2018. Available at: http://divulgacandcontas.tse.jus.br/candidaturas/oficial/2018/BR/BR/2022802018/280000614517/proposta_1534284632231.pdf.

Castro, Celso. *General Villas Bôas: conversa com o comandante*. Rio de Janeiro: Editora da Fundação Getúlio Vargas, 2021.

Cervo, Amado and Bueno, Clodoaldo. *História da Política Exterior do Brasil*. Brasília: Editora da Unb, 2002.

Dieguez, Consuelo. "O Chanceler do Regresso". *Revista Piauí*, Edition 151, April 2019.

Frazão, Fernando. "O influenciador digital de Pequim na polarização". *O Estado de São Paulo*, April 11, 2020.

Gomes Filho, Paulo Roberto da Silva. Interview to the author. October 22, 2021.

Lapper, Richard. "Bolsonaro took aim at China". Then reality struck. *Americas Quarterly*, Volume 13, Issue 2, 2019.

Li, Yang. "Valorize as relações Brasil-China, deputado Eduardo". *O Globo*, April 4, 2020.

Mainwaring, Scott, Meneguello, Raquel, and Power, Timothy. *Partidos Conservadores no Brasil Contemporâneo*. São Paulo: Editora Paz e Terra, 2000.

Maklouf Carvalho, Luiz. *O Cadete e o Capitão: a vida de Jair Bolsonaro no quartel*. São Paulo: Todavia, 2019.

Martin, Peter. *China's Civilian Army: The making of wolf warrior diplomacy*. Oxford: Oxford University Press, 2021.

Mello, Patrícia Campos. "Itamaraty abafa diplomacia da máscara, e doações chinesas emperram por logística." *Folha de São Paulo*, June 17, 2020.

Oliveira, Henrique Altemani de. "Brasil-China: trinta anos de uma parceria estratégica". *Revista Brasileira de Política Internacional*, Volume 47, Issue 1, 2004.

Pires, Carol. "Retrato Narrado", 2020. Podcast: https://piaui.folha.uol.com.br/retrato-narrado/.

Rosa, Bruno. "As estatais chinesas que chamaram a atenção no leilão do pré-sal". *Época*, November 6, 2019.

Safatle, Claudia, Borges, João and Oliveira, Ribamar. *Anatomia de um desastre: Os bastidores da crise econômica que mergulhou o país na pior recessão da história*. São Paulo: Portfolio-Penguin, 2016.

Santoro, Maurício. "Lições Pandêmicas sobre as Relações Brasil-China". *JOTA Info*, July 1, 2021.

———. "Bolsonaros' troubled relationship with China". *Diálogo Chino*, March 26, 2020.

———. "Mourão ganha protagonismo com viagem à China". *Revista Época*, May 26, 2019.

———. "Bolsonaro's Diplomacy: Three groups clash for foreign policy control". *Brazilian Report*, April 1, 2019.

———. "A Gafe de Bolsonaro". *O Globo*, March 14, 2018.

Sedgwick, Mark. *Key thinkers of the radical right*. Oxford: Oxford University Press, 2019.

Senra, Ricardo. "Um ano após reclamar que China 'compraria o Brasil', Bolsonaro quer vender estatais e commodities em visita a Xi Jinping". *BBC Brasil*, October 23, 2019.

Spektor, Matias. *Azeredo da Silveira: um depoimento*. Rio de Janeiro: Editora da Fundação Getúlio Vargas, 2010.

Teitelbaum, Benjamin. *War for eternity: Inside Bannon's far right circle of global power brokers*. New York: HarperCollins, 2020.

Traumann, Thomas. "58% dos brasileiros têm visão favorável aos EUA e 44% rejeitam a China". *Veja*, October 5, 2021.

Vigevani, Tullo, Oliveira, Marcelo, and Cintra, Rodrigo. "Política Externa no Período FHC: a busca de autonomia pela integração." *Revista Brasileira de Política Internacional*, Volume 15, Issue 2, 2003.

Vizentini, Paulo. *A Política Externa do Regime Militar Brasileiro*. Porto Alegre: Editora da UFRGS, 1998.

William, Wagner. *A Operação Secreta Etiópia-Maranhão: a guerra dos respiradores no ano da pandemia*. São Paulo: Vestígio, 2021.

Winter, Brian. "System profile: Behind the rise of Jair Bolsonaro". *Americas Quarterly*, Volume 11, Issue 1, 2018.

CONCLUSION

Brazil and China began their conversation almost five centuries ago, when the first Portuguese caravels returning from Guangzhou and Macao stopped in Rio de Janeiro and brought tea, silk, porcelain and other products from the Far East. Their modern relationship is younger, starting in 1974, when the Brazilian generals running the military regime understood that with the rapprochement with the United States the PRC was becoming an important global player.

Over the last five decades, Brazil and China first imagined their dialogue as a partnership between two developing nations with critical positions concerning the industrialized West. Brasília and Beijing realized they could support each other in multilateral organizations and even in ambitious scientific and technologic projects, such as building satellites together. In the first twenty years of their new relationship, they step by step established a framework for their diplomacy, slowly overcoming the initial cautious approach of the Brazilian military dictatorship.

In the 1990s, Brazil and China developed the innovative concept of "strategic partnership", a flexible arrangement which pointed to a commitment to both Brasília and Beijing, in the sense of realizing that their relationship was important as a long-term goal, and not just immediate concerns over trade. However, the idea took ten years to really bear fruit.

The watershed moment was the global commodity boom of the 2000s, when the bilateral trade skyrocketed and the PRC became Brazil's top

© The Editor(s) (if applicable) and The Author(s), under exclusive
license to Springer Nature Singapore Pte Ltd. 2022
M. Santoro, *Brazil–China Relations in the 21st Century*,
https://doi.org/10.1007/978-981-19-0353-3

trade partner. China also started to invest strongly in South America, especially in energy and mining, turning itself into an important source of financial resources for Brazil. The decade coincided with left-wing governments in Brasília, which saw Beijing as an ally in a series of multilateral coalitions aimed at the reform of international organizations—G20, BRICS, BASIC. They were a form of "soft balancing"—i.e., non-military—from the Global South, in contrast with the established positions of the West.

Nonetheless, the rapid Chinese growth transformed the strategic partnership in a way that they creators could not have imagined. The PRC grew so much that it became richer and more powerful than Brazil, and trade patterns turned into an asymmetric exchange of Brazilian commodities from Chinese manufactured goods, adding concerns for Brazil's industrialists, already worried about the decline of industry in the country after the crisis of the national-developmentalist model of the 1930–1980s.

When Brazilian faced a series of political and economic crises in the 2010s, there were many in the country who believed that the PRC was part of the problem. An anti-China discourse was an important part of the diplomatic agenda of a new nationalist right movement which rose fast in the wake of scandals and recessions, reaching power through the presidential elections. This group searched for a special relation with Washington and harshly criticized the Chinese political system.

Although it did not end the strategic partnership, it introduced new tensions in the bilateral relationship. For the first time since the Cold War, the PRC became a controversial partisan issue in Brazil, opposing the president and local authorities, such as governors, who were quick to exploit the opportunity for a direct dialogue with Beijing, especially in the dire circumstances of the coronavirus pandemic.

The road ahead points to stronger economic ties, with rising trade and investment, and a more complex web of political interests. The PRC is more concerned with climate change and deforestation of tropical rainforest, a course which may create partnerships with Brazil, but also sometimes provoke tensions, due to the erratic trajectory of the Brazilian presidential administrations regarding these subjects. New technologies, from artificial intelligence to the 5G Internet pattern or renewable energies, are also becoming more important to the bilateral dialogues.

A rising China is putting efforts in understanding Latin America, creating specialists to work with the region. In that regard, Brazil is far behind. After three decades of the strategic partnership, the country still lacks basic expertise in dealing with the PRC, counting much more on personal initiatives and individual interests than on national public policies to respond to the new Chinese role in the world.

The bilateral relationship is also asymmetrical in terms of knowledge, for the PRC usually has more information about Brazil than the opposite. In general terms, the Chinese know better what they want from Brazilians, who often have vague and generic aspirations on how to benefit from China's rise, but without detailed plans on how to achieve these gains.

In an international context of growing tensions between China and the West, Brazil's diplomacy towards the PRC will be increasingly under pressure on how the country will position itself concerning issues such as the South China sea disputes, or conflicts regarding Xinjiang or Hong Kong. The strategic partnership with Beijing is not isolated from other relationships in Brazilian foreign policy, especially with traditional partners such as the United States or the European Union.

Appendix: List of Interviews

1. Gilberto Câmara, former director of the Brazilian Institute of Space Research (Inpe). Geneva, June 14th, 2021.
2. Jaime Spitcovsky, former correspondent in Beijing. São Paulo, July 12th, 2021.
3. Welber Barral, former secretary of Foreign Trade. Brasília, July 23rd, 2021.
4. Tatiana Prazeres, former secretary of Foreign Trade. Beijing, July 27th, 2021.
5. Charles Tang, chairman of the Brazil-China Chamber of Trade and Industry, Rio de Janeiro, September 10th, 2021.
6. Margaret Myers, director of the Asia and Latin American Program, Inter-American Dialogue. Washington, September 13th, 2021.
7. Paulo Menechelli, researcher, Porto Alegre, September 17th, 2021.
8. Qiao Jinzghen, former director of Confucius Institute in Rio de Janeiro. Shijiazhuang, September 23th, 2021.
9. Milena de Moura, movie director. São Paulo, September 27th, 2021.
10. Paulo Roberto da Silva Gomes Filho, retired colonel of the Brazilian Army. Brasília, October 22th, 2021.
11. Celso Amorim, former minister of Foreign Affairs and former minister of Defense. Teresópolis, October 30th, 2021.

12. Natalie Unterstell, diretor Tanaloa Institute, former climate negotiator for Brazil. Rio de Janeiro, December 17th, 2021.
13. Ana Cândida Perez, former Brazilian consul-general in Shanghai. Rio de Janeiro, December 27th, 2021.
14. Luiz Augusto Castro Neves, former Brazilian ambassador to Beijing. Rio de Janeiro, December 28th, 2021.

Index

116 INDEX

Panama, 25, 26
Pandemic, xiv, 30, 52, 57, 90, 97–102, 106
Pará, 53, 75, 76, 78
Paradiplomacy, 98, 99
Paraguay, 25
Paris Agreement, 83–85, 95
People's Daily, 63
People's Liberation Army (PLA), 94
People's Republic of China (PRC), xi–xiii, 1–7, 12, 21, 26, 31, 37, 39, 60, 61, 92, 94, 105–107
Pepper, 21, 72
Perez, Ana Cândida, 31
Peru, 24, 25, 82
Petrobras, 11, 40, 49, 58, 91, 97
Politburo, 11
Populist, 90, 91, 93, 102
Porcelain, 25, 105
Portugal, 32, 56, 64
Portugal, Ricardo, 61
Portuguese, 9, 14, 25, 26, 29, 39, 56, 61, 72, 74, 99, 105
Poverty, 9, 35, 65, 83
Prazeres, Tatiana, 32, 35, 38, 58
Programa de Parceria de Investimentos, 54

Q

Qian, Qichen, 13
Qiao, Jianzhen, 61

R

Railways, xi, 47, 53, 54, 56, 76, 77, 97
Raw materials, xiii, 17, 21, 24, 48
Recession, xii, 11, 22, 29, 50, 84, 89–91, 97, 102, 106
Reform and opening, 1, 16, 29, 34, 60

Rio de Janeiro, xi, 12, 61, 74, 91, 100, 101, 105
Rousseff, Dilma, 38, 91
Rua da Alfândega, 62
Rua Vinte e Cinco de Março, 25
Rubber, 32, 71, 73, 81
Russia, 14, 17, 40, 54, 63

S

Santos, Lucélia, 64
São Paulo, xi, 6, 12–15, 25, 60, 63, 91, 98–100
Sarney, José, 8, 10
Satellites, xii, xiii, 1, 9, 10, 17, 21, 105
Shanghai, 29, 31, 58, 98
Si Lao, 62
Silk, 25, 105
Silveira, Antônio Azeredo da, 3, 4, 7
Silver, 25
Sino-Brazilian, xi, xii, 3, 6, 8, 9, 11, 13, 24, 29–31, 35, 39, 40, 51, 55, 60, 64, 65, 71, 72, 89, 90, 96–98, 101
Sobral Pinto, Heráclito, 5
South Africa, 16, 40, 78, 82
South America, 11, 15, 21, 23, 29, 49, 55, 57, 85, 98, 106
South Korea, 11, 65, 92
Soy, 22, 26, 30, 32–34, 48, 74, 75, 79, 96
Soybean, xi, xiii, 32–35, 54, 63, 71, 74–76, 78–81, 84, 98, 101
Soybean moratorium, 79
Spanish, 25, 26
Spitzcovsky, Jaime, 11, 14, 15, 17, 58, 63
Standing committee, 11
State Grid, 7, 15, 55, 56, 58, 76
State-owned enterprise (SOE), 7, 11, 40, 51, 53, 54, 56–59, 76, 78, 95, 97

Z
Zhang, Daqian, 60
Zhang, Yimou, 60

Zhao, Zyiang, 12
Zhu, Ronji, 12, 13

Made in the USA
Middletown, DE
22 August 2024